HATE

A PROGRESSIVE DISEASE

TRESTE LOVING

Published by Motivational Press, Inc.
1777 Aurora Road
Melbourne, Florida, 32935
www.MotivationalPress.com

Manufactured in the United States of America.

ISBN: 978-1-62865-561-2

CONTENTS

ACKNOWLEDGEMENTS   **5**

INTRODUCTION   **6**

CHAPTER

What You Need To Know *7*

CHAPTER 2

Back to the Future *19*

CHAPTER 3

Man overboard! *26*

CHAPTER 4

I would not save you! *37*

CHAPTER 5

Get Your Paper Right Here *48*

CHAPTER 6

Imagine His Surprise *57*

CHAPTER 7

Wrong Conversations? *67*

CHAPTER 8

Seriously, is that the only seat? *76*

CHAPTER 9

Extremists May Be In Your Town Right Now *84*

CHAPTER 10

Hate *97*

CHAPTER 11

"I have 10 African-American friends" *106*

CHAPTER 12

It's A Right-Handed World *110*

CHAPTER 13

Perception *114*

CHAPTER 14

The Others *117*

CHAPTER

What Disguise Do You Wear? *120*

CHAPTER 16

'Let's Be Real!' *124*

CHAPTER 17

Bag It *127*

AND FINALLY...   **129**

ACKNOWLEDGEMENTS

THANK YOU IS NOT ENOUGH to say to my husband Scott, my Aunt Katie, other family and friends for their consistent support and reminding me I had great stories worth reading and some bold answers to overcome hate. They kept me going when I sometimes felt I was going to nowhere with this book. Thank you and bless all of you always!! I love you all immensely!

INTRODUCTION

"**I** CAN'T WORK FOR NIGGERS!" he said as he bursts into my office. Bias leads to stereotypes, prejudices, racism, sexism, Islamophobia, and so much more. We all have biases it's time, to be honest. I know hate drudges up some powerful emotions and even some denial. Some might say, "I don't hate anyone. I just love my own more." Sounds good but doesn't change the fact that people hate. Hate is a strong word. Hate is not going anywhere.

It is not easy to confront hate, but there are some ways that I've used that have worked. My actual experiences will give you pause to think. Start by stepping out and speaking up when you hear or see hate in progress. "Excuse me, why did you just say/do that?" "What does that mean?" How does hate start and why is it seemingly impossible to change a hater's mind? You'll understand how our socialization makes us who we are including behaviors, beliefs, hate, traditions, values, language, culture, and everything else.

I thought this book was a bit strong with language and the idea of hate. It's not. In 2017 a Caucasian teacher allegedly called some fourth-grade African-American students rats. Additionally, a Caucasian teacher pulled an African-American child, by his arm, through a hallway. There are so many more incidents, unfortunately. And yes, there are African-Americans who hate Caucasians andI discuss that in this book.

Hate distorts everything. Hate is a progressive disease. Find a cure in this book.

CHAPTER 1

What You Need To Know

I F WE TEACH OUR KIDS by example then we only have ourselves to blame. This chapter is for readers to understand terms and concepts throughout the book.

We are born as blank pieces of paper no biases. Socialization is the root of who we are; it's the primary way we learn our cultures through an all-encompassing educational process. One generation passes to the next everything that makes their family who they are, unique. The process is the same for all of us the difference is the content we receive. There two types of socialization natural and deliberate. Natural occurs during our baby to early infant timeframe when we discover the world and how it affects us. Deliberate socialization is how we obtain our values, beliefs, customs, attitudes, and all other attributes that define a culture and will create a person's identity. Think about it: when I joined the Navy that was a different world. Boot camp was the socialization process I went through to become a Sailor. I sometimes felt scared and lost, but I remembered who I was and went back to what I knew through my socialization.

There are influences on the socialization process and knowing these help people understand each other and ourselves. The most influential agent of socialization is the family. The family includes immediate and far family, i.e. cousins, aunts, and uncles. Etiquette, religion, prejudices, behaviors, language, values, attitudes, and much more comes from family.

Family is slowly becoming the second most influence on us as we are socialized. Currently, the second influence is the media and technology. Here are some facts that demonstrate how each culture is unique through socialization.

Hispanic and Latino are not interchangeable ethnic terms. Hispanic is about language, speaking Spanish, and Latino is about geography. For example, if someone is from Colombia is Hispanic, they speak Spanish and Latino because they are from Latin America. But someone from Brazil is only Latino because they speak Portuguese in Brazil. Those ethnic groups span the races, white to black. People misuse the word Hispanic as though it is a race. These are important distinctions to help us interact with these folks.

The media has become a major influence on many folks. Media includes TV, movies, 24-hour news cycle, newspapers, video games, radio, and much more. This influence can, of course, be positive or negative. The negative influences are the ones that create conflict. One example is movies and TV will reinforce negative stereotypes by casting people in stereotypical roles. Blacks are usually thieves, murders, and narcotics dealers. Hispanics are uneducated and live a life of crime. Here's another common stereotype in movies Italian Americans who are mobsters. There is much evidence that many Italian Americans were mobsters when they first came to this country but not all Italian Americans were mobsters. All tigers are cats but not all cats are tigers, explained a bit later. I've seen and heard those stereotypes from movies and the news cycles which rarely show minorities in a positive light. Unfortunately, even Asian Pacific Islanders are usually in stereotypical roles. They are cast as martial arts stars or in sub-servient roles. One important thing to note here is how Caucasian males are portrayed in movies or TV. They are right, powerful, and the one who saves the day. Additionally, the 24-hour news cycle reinforce negative stereotypes because of the stories they highlight. Murder is more interesting than a school board meeting. Are there any positive stories about minorities out there?

Technology. People can go on the internet, even while walking or driving, and find anything including hate websites. Why is that important? When hate data is right in someone's face, some will pay attention. Additionally, during the socialization process, young adults whose primary interaction with the world is through games may have issues relating to those portrayed negatively in some games. From technology to, religion, friends, teachers, and the school environment all are important influencers outside the family for the socialization process.

We see how religion still plays an important part of the United States culture. Churches are some of the most segregated places in the U.S. It has always been that way and shows very little change. However, there are many that are integrated and are thriving. Church integration has a profound impact on socialization. Religion is sometimes more complicated than we tend to think. For instance, Islam is a religion of peace and love according to their Qur'an. Unfortunately, there are Islamic extremists who have misused the Qur'an and are socializing people who know very little about Islam. Some religious socialization is almost as influential, if not more influential, as family.

Friends' influence over us comes in a plethora of ways. A clique is one of the most common ways friends influence us. Being part of a clique in the socialization process we give up who we are to adopt what the clique is about. ISIS can be viewed as a terrorist clique and is very effective in socializing people thousands of miles away through technology, the internet. Other cliques are Christians, baseball players, meaning that all cliques are not bad but they all operate the same way. Cliques can be disruptive to an individual's socialization because folks use the accepted group norm whether it is what an individual may think or believe.

Teachers also influence the socialization process by their teaching style and how they treat their students. I see teachers as a rising influence on their students' socialization. The school environment changes as society changes. What is becoming more frequent in some schools is that a teacher will treat a minority student much different than a Caucasian student. Here's an example of how that occurs in a classroom. A Caucasian teacher believes that minority students are not as competent as their white students. Therefore, the teachers expect less from, spend less time with, and provide less assistance to minority students. Those students perform the way the teacher expects. A teacher may not even notice what's happened. Young adults will suffer from this classroom socialization.

Understanding the socialization process helps folks figure out who they are so they can comfortably meet those who do not look like them.

So how does one interact with people who are not like them and not compromise oneself?

Stay true. Personal beliefs are just that, personal. Share what you consider positive attributes.

Unfortunately, minorities are not always seen as positive contributors to society. We've witnessed some compelling stories about minorities making a difference. For example, Malala Yousafzai, who demanded girls be educated, was shot in the head by a Taliban gunman in 2012 and went on to win a Noble Peace prize at 18 years old. She is the youngest person ever to become a Noble Prize laureate. She's fearless. Fear can stop people from doing the right thing, but it feels good when action is taken.

Next, silence is consent, the opposite of acting. When cultures collide, it can be uncomfortable and that makes it hard to question a person's behavior. If a person doesn't step up, the person appears to be going along with whatever negative things are happening. I've been in this situation but was able to confront the behaviors and sometimes they changed. To be honest, I didn't always step up and confront the wrong being done. It was a delicate dance because I was going against what they were taught by family, religion, friends, etc. So, I was speaking against everything they stood for in their life. No one wants to have their mother or religion portrayed as being wrong. However, there doesn't have to be conflict when offering a different perspective. My different perspective doesn't mean I was right or wrong, it is just another way to see or handle a tense situation. I've also done nothing, and it was detrimental. Fear can keep us silent.

Next, Unconscious Bias (Implicit Bias) allows people to say and do things to others that appear to be perfectly fine. Unconscious Bias is a result of our socialization which causes us to make snap decisions and assessments of people and situations. These are called microaggressions. Microaggressions was coined by Psychologist Derald Sue, PhD a Columbia University professor and they are brief everyday slights, insults, indignities and denigrating messages sent to people of color by well-meaning White people unaware of the hidden messages. Here are examples of microaggressions, *"Is that your real hair?"* Or, *"You don't act black."*

I still don't know what "act Black" means. My real-life experiences with my Caucasian husband when we go certain places for dinner turns into a microaggression. When it's time to pay for the meal, we must tell the cashier or hostess we are together. They didn't ask the white couples before us. Those microaggressions are hard to ignore and my husband notices them right away, so it doesn't only affect me. That was a good way to communicate they did not see me with him. Another example, my husband and I went to a small town, island, for a visit, and we ate lunch at a restaurant. Some people cared less, although there were some stares. One lady was sitting rather close to us, and she was staring at me, not just taking a glimpse. I've been in this situation before, so I knew what would stop the staring. I said hi and asked her if I was wearing her blouse. Of course, she went back to her food and my husband and I enjoyed our meal in peace.

Microaggressions can and have sometimes done irreparable damage to many people. When one does happen, the behavior that prompted it must be identified immediately and pointed out. Correction can be something as simple as pointing out the behavior that others don't recognize or when suspected behavior is intentional then a firmer objection is warranted. My example above with the restaurant behavior exhibited by the woman was unmistakably overt in nature and as such should or could be addressed similarly to what I did or even more bluntly. Implicit bias is not new; it is being called out due to many racially related incidents. The U.S. is more diverse than ever so confronting these types of behaviors is important. Next, it's time to discuss stereotypes.

We all have stereotypes ergo we all have prejudices. Prejudice is an irrational attitude of hostility directed against an individual, a group, a race, or their supposed characteristics. Stereotypes are to believe unfairly that all people or things with a particular characteristic are the same. I love this next saying because it speaks to stereotypes: All tigers are cats but all cats are not tigers. It is said there are good stereotypes. However, those are just rationalizations using microaggressions. These rationalizations cause people to come up with these so-called 'exceptions' because evidence leads to incongruence or inconsistencies of what they had believed through their socialization leading to the stereotype.

Here's a stereotype I've heard, "Caucasians are racists and keep minorities down, so we can't be entirely successful." Not true. Some minorities believe that statement. Here's the thing about Caucasians, they can totally ignore minorities when they desire so some care less about minorities and their lives. Therefore, when Caucasians come into contact with minorities they feel uncomfortable and their stereotypes kick-in. Remember, all tigers are cats but not all cats are tigers.

On the other hand, it's difficult for minorities to ignore Caucasians because there are limited businesses or places that are totally for minorities. So, we, minorities, are always conscious of our behaviors because a stereotype happens easily. When was the last time you heard about a Caucasian being pulled over by the police for 'driving while Caucasian'? That is called privilege and is discussed later. But, we all know that police have stopped minorities in 'the wrong neighborhood' and asked why they were there. Once again, all tigers are cats but not all cats are tigers.

Prejudices in action are discrimination. Discrimination is an act that leads to treating people different because they belong to an outgroup, which describes all minorities. The definition of the outgroup may soon change. The Latino/Hispanic ethnic groups are growing and has made some serious inroads in many states, and they are expected to be the majority group in the U.S. between the years of 2030 and 2050.

Two more concepts that are vital to understanding the rest of this book are diversity and inclusion.

Diversity and Inclusion (D/I) are two words that people have heard quite a lot about but, there are still misconceptions about what they mean. Diversity means different. It is all our various dimensions that make us who we are: unique. Everyone knows the most common aspects we all possess such as race, ethnicity, age, religion, sex, and more. However, we are more than just those few dimensions. Analytical abilities, intellectual discipline, thinking styles, where a person is from, and much more makes us an entirely whole person different from any other.

Inclusion is creating an environment where everyone is welcome, respected, and encouraged to get involved. Inclusion is what makes diversity awesome and work.

I've heard diversity called equal opportunity (EO) in disguise, or it is code for Affirmative Action (AA). If the only dimensions people concentrate on are the obvious ones, i.e. race and sex, then I understand their skepticism. But diversity is not code for anything other than diversity. Above I gave the expanded definition of diversity which should make it clear that it is unlike anything. Affirmative Action's intent is to allow the organization to promote and hire qualified minorities in positions they normally are not considered to fill. Unfortunately, organizations used AA the wrong way, and it turned out to be a quota system. Equal opportunity is part of diversity, as far as descriptive dimensions, but EO concerns more. EO ensures equitable treatment regardless of who you are, what you look like, or where you live. Later in this book I'll write a lot about the Navy, so next I'll provide some useful information.

It is helpful to know 'jargon' and some general Navy policies and procedures and rank. First, I was on an aircraft carrier, and that is a different world. An aircraft carrier is a floating city. There are over 5,000 Sailors and civilians aboard the carrier when on a deployment. Here are some relevant data about the carrier: the length is 1,092 feet, 257 feet wide, it is 244 feet high, displaces approximately 97,000 tons and most importantly we all worked, ate, and slept together, in close quarters, for months on deployment. We were usually out to sea and during a one-year period, on the USS George Washington (CVN 73), we were underway over 240 days. That alone created an environment that was perfect for issues to arise and people's true colors were exposed. Although we had port calls, port visits, we still were together because of our rules in port. Port calls happened about every 30-45 days when possible. Working, sleeping and spending 24 hours a day seven days a week working in close quarters can bring out the worst in some. There had to be some way to handle the issues born from our environment. The Navy has their own discipline and punishment systems. On the carrier, there are a few different disciplinary items that are more effective out at sea than using them onshore. Those processes are tightly monitored through Navy lawyers, on both sides, and an appeal process. Part of my job responsibilities was to provide Sailors with Navy Regulations that applied to their situation and gave them information on how the appeal process works. I also provided the chain of command with violations Sailors had committed so I had to be a twin. Sometimes I was the good guy, but mostly I was the villain. I was a villain because I ensured everyone, regardless of their rank or position, were held to the same standard, Navy regulations. *Assuring accountability and equitable treatment.* Additionally, I assured victims of discrimination, sexual assault, and sexual harassment knew their rights and responsibilities to have their case adjudicated. Being a trusted advisor who reported directly to Commanding Officer (CO), the boss, I always had to be on top of my game. I reported to directly to the Executive Officer, XO, on a daily basis.

Rank structure is necessary to understand because that made the difference on who I talked to, how I spoke to them, and when I engaged them in my process. I was an E-8, Senior Chief Petty Officer, one below the most senior rank for enlisted Sailors.

It was imperative to create trust with both the chain of command and the Sailors so when someone needed my help they knew I was available to them. I was very visible to everyone. I did get some issues that were not illegal but needed attention because others' actions were not in keeping with the highest standards of the Navy. These types of concerns occur daily in the business world.

I had some intense training for 16 weeks to be certified as an Equal Opportunity Advisor/Diversity Officer (EOA/ DO) and I figured out that this job is for me. The intensity of the training prepared me for all the cases I received. A skill I was taught, "keep my bag closed", was critical to being successful as an EOA/DO. My bag is where I put my prejudices, represented by rocks. So, I tightly closed my bag and put it away therefore I could talk to anyone about anything. These situations were not as easy as I make them sound, but I was prepared. Chapter 17 covers more about the bag.

Here's one example of what I dealt with on the carrier. We were in our homeport, and I was wrapping up my day, it's 1745 or 5:45 pm, there are only a few of us onboard the ship. Just as I was about to leave, a junior Sailor came to my office. I thought it had been a long day, but the Sailor was very upset. I couldn't ask him to wait until tomorrow. This young man, about 19 years old, had tears in his eyes, and he was shaking. He told me his division chief, supervisor, sent him to me so I could hear it from the Sailor himself.

I told him to start from the beginning with as much detail as possible. He, I'll call him Frank, took a couple of deep breaths and began to describe his horrible situation. He was scared. I told him to relax, and he finally stopped shaking. Frank said Marty, his division officer, was calling him names in front of everyone in his division. He added that Marty had threatened to toss him off the ship when we were at sea and turn our gun mount and shoot him until he was dead. I had to take a minute to replay what he just told me. I gathered my thoughts and asked Frank how many times this has occurred. He said at least five times. One time was bad enough, but Marty's brain seemed to be stuck on Frank and scaring him. Marty's behaviors appeared to be a way for him to lead by intimidation. Frank happened to be the example. Fortunately, there were a few others in Frank's division that were willing to talk to me, and I asked them what they saw and heard. They confirmed what Frank said, and they thought Frank had suffered. I had Frank write a statement as accurately as possible. In the meantime, I called his division chief, and we talked. We'll call his division chief David, he and I talked outside my office about this situation while Frank was writing his statement. David told me he was there every time Marty debased Frank. It was David's job to stop this, but he was intimidated by Marty as well. However, David also wrote a statement because he knew something had to be done. I was upset, but not at David. I didn't know Marty, but his actions were criminal and abusive. I checked to see if my CO was still onboard because of the seriousness of this issue and Marty's rank. Marty was prior enlisted, like me, but he was selected to be an officer. He knew how his actions would really shake Frank. Fortunately, the CO was still onboard. I collected their written statements and had them follow me to the CO's office. I went in first to tell him why I was there, and he read the statements. He talked to both Frank and David. The CO was angry and disappointed by Marty's actions. Our CO was a fair, strict, reasonable, personable commander and both Frank and Marty would receive fair and equitable treatment.

Marty was still onboard, and the CO called him to his office. I sent Frank and David back to their office and told them not to leave until they heard from me. It was the CO, Marty and me. It was quick. The CO asked Marty if what his Sailors said was true. Marty said yes. Marty said he was only joking with Frank and everyone knew that but Frank. The

CO told him to get off his ship, and he didn't want to see Marty again. Marty looked at me as though he wanted to choke me, but I wasn't scared. I made sure Frank and David left before Marty. Frank left but David stayed to talk to Marty. Marty had no idea that David had started this whole ball rolling. I finally wrapped up what I could do until tomorrow and as I was leaving, I saw Marty leaving. He had to take everything that belonged to him off the ship that day. We bring aboard what we need for our deployments and keep a lot of it on the ship while in port. So, he had a lot to move at once. He stopped walking and glared at me. I didn't give in to his attempt to intimidate me, although he was a scary guy. I kept walking with my head up and my usual bright, inviting smile. Why did Marty believe he could bully people? Marty was about 6'3", weighed maybe 250, and very muscular, making him imposing. He usually had a scowl on his face to further intimidate. Marty did think he got the last shot at me. He told David I should have kept my nose out of his business, I was a fucking bitch, and I'm lucky. He thought I would crumble or something I guess, but I replied to David my favorite word I used on the ship to help me keep sane...whatever!

Finally, the basics are complete. I gave more than enough for you to enjoy this book without even being in the Navy. The next five actual cases cover six years of my eighteen years of experience. Three cases are about racists and my accounts of those interviews. One case is about discrimination allegations. One case is about harassment and his desperate attempt to get away. All my racist's cases involve men. Through my research and experience of hate groups, their membership is overwhelmingly male. Through my 24 years of experience, approximately 98% of alleged offenders I dealt with were male. The Navy's Equal Opportunity/Diversity strategies are robust and progressive and that's why I decided to do this job as long as I could. Let's get into this and enjoy!

CHAPTER 2

Back to the Future

"**I** can't do this anymore!"

Abe had an intimidating appearance. He was 6'2", blonde, blue eyes, very trim and fit, and a huge red and blue star tattoo on the side of his neck. Abe was soft spoken and extremely friendly, so he did not intimidate me. He approached me to ask a serious question and was a bit concerned about my answer. Because I conducted training for all new Sailors and key people as part of getting to know the ship, those young Sailors knew me. My training was extensive, especially about hate groups. The tattoos and graffiti were the highlights of my training. I had actual examples of tattoos and graffiti from onboard the ship, so it was interesting and a bit eye opening for some people. There were tons of questions, and I liked it because they were listening, and their curiosity was promising.

Abe's reaction to my training was interesting. Of course, I saw his star, so I figured he had a great story, but I was not ready for all he said. Abe said he had quite a few tattoos, and he wanted to show me before someone else came to me. During my training, I asked everyone to keep their eyes open for tattoos and graffiti and report it to me because I could not be everywhere. That request made a lot of people uncomfortable looking at others for tattoos, but a few of them did, and their help was invaluable. Abe was a bit nervous with me initially, so I started our conversation with easy questions. I asked him where he was from, why he joined the Navy and a few questions about his family. Once he was more at ease, I asked him to tell me about any hate groups he belonged to before joining the Navy and if he was currently in any hate group. Abe opened right up, and I was intrigued by his story. He was in a hate group for about six years before joining the Navy but, he was not currently in a hate group. I left that part of the conversation to focus on his tattoos. He had many other tattoos, so we started with his star and then checked out the rest of them. Tattoos talk to those who see them, and they say many different things depending on who is viewing them. Just like a name tag or billboard ad, you can recognize people and what they believe in without asking questions. Tattoos are the same and when they are hate group related they can be intimidating. They are also an acknowledgment of belonging to a group. Not everyone is well versed in identifying tattoos, and neither was I until I did some serious research. My research took me to websites that are horrible with their words toward minorities. However, I learned so much I didn't know, and it helped me when talking to people with tattoos, racists, and those who either saw the tattoos or told me about them. I incorporated my experiences to help others be up to date on the status of hate on the aircraft carrier. I also added it to my research into my welcome aboard training.

Abe was surprised at my knowledge about tattoos and extremist groups which made him feel even more comfortable in our conversations. He told me as soon as he got out of the hate group he joined the Navy. I affirmed his positive decisions. Abe described to me how he felt about African-Americans, and it was not pretty. When he was speaking, I felt a slight hint of dislike toward Abe. However, I knew my job, so I kept "my bag closed" and moved on. After speaking with Abe for about two hours, he came to a decision. Abe asked me if I could help him change, get rid of the hate. He wanted to speak privately at least once a week and discuss how he might be able to change his feelings. To be truthful with Abe I told him I could not help him change his feelings, but I could provide some techniques to change his perspectives. We also agreed that he could come to me more often if he had an urge to talk. I was elated yet a bit hesitant because Abe would be the first person I would try to help personally, one-on-one, who was an admitted racist.

Abe and I started from the beginning. I asked him why he hated African-Americans and no other minorities which usually is not the case. Most hate groups hate all minorities or people of color. He told me what he said he knew. African-Americans are lazy, they fight, they steal, they are always high on drugs, they sell drugs and much more. That's how he was socialized, and unfortunately, Abe took it to be true. Even though he had had a few positive interactions with African-Americans, he had far more negative interactions. Abe joined the Navy soon after he graduated from high school. He looked at joining the Navy for a possible fresh start. When we talked, Abe had a sense of humor, easy to talk to, and brilliant. I thoroughly enjoyed talking with him. Our conversations were the first time he had spoken to an African-American person in-depth. Before meeting me, Abe said he wasn't interested in knowing any African-Americans.

Our conversations were honest. Abe started to relax and enjoy our discussions about African-Americans in general. But we talked about more than race. I tried to mentor him about the Navy and guide him through difficult times outside race. I knew I couldn't change Abe's beliefs and attitudes toward African-American people but I wanted to give him a new perspective, which could change his behaviors. Realizing I couldn't change people, offering them a new perspective was reasonable. Having much success with others, on easier topics, I used that success when speaking with Abe. However, I knew that a small amount of time with me would not have a lasting perspective change. He had at least 18 years of thinking, learning, and hearing about African-Americans' and our behaviors. Abe began to come to me when he felt his old feelings start coming back, especially when he felt like fighting an African-American male. He was set off by African-American males even for little things they did. Abe and I talked through these situations, and when we finished, he seemed calmer. I wouldn't go so far as to say Abe trusted me, but I believe he felt I would be honest with him regardless of the outcome. I must say some of these conversations were difficult for me. Not because of how Abe felt, but because it drained me having these conversations. I had to think about what to say and I was using active listening. *Active listening*

is as its name states. An active listener repeats, paraphrases, nods their head, maintains the proper non-verbal behaviors and much more. Mental exhaustion creates physical exhaustion when active listening. My desire to help Abe caused me to search myself and my feelings about his negative comments. Past experiences taught me to at least try to make a situation better. Even though I may not totally believe what I'm saying to someone will change anything about their thinking, including Abe,

it was worth my effort, so I do it anyway. *Things that I didn't personally agree with I had to confront and give the appropriate answer. So, I kept my bag closed.* That was not an easy task when I was dealing with things that create conflict. I knew this when I volunteered for this position as Equal Opportunity Advisor. Maintaining my composure during racially charged situations was one of the behaviors I hoped others would adopt.

I didn't just have to deal with Abe; issues were consistently arising that I had to confront. There were days I only slept three or four hours, then I was up again the next day, unsure of what would come my way. I began getting complaints about racial graffiti in the heads, (bathrooms), in passageways, (halls), even underneath racks, (beds). The racks are stacked three high that means the bottom of one rack is the top of another's rack. I could never find all the graffiti because there was so much. I'll cover graffiti more in depth in Chapter 4. Abe had started doing graffiti on his rack. I only knew because he showed me. It was not the worst I'd seen, but it was troubling. After seeing the graffiti, Abe and I had a conversation, initiated by me. He talked, and I listened, I talked, and he listened. During these conversations, it dawned on me that my expectations for Abe's behavior may have been too high. Our desires were slightly incongruent. Things were about to get unsettling. He told me that he heard about some possible extremist activities both while onboard the ship and when on liberty, free time away from the ship. I pretty much knew what he was going to tell me next. Abe confirmed he had started hanging out with these guys. That behavior is what Abe knew. However, I could sense his turmoil, and I hated to see that. My relationship with Abe started changing.

Now I was just a sounding board for Abe. He didn't ask me so many questions about how he could change. Nor did he seem to care about what we'd done and how far he had come. So, I didn't entirely give up on Abe because I thought it was worth my time to possibly get him away from extremist talk and behavior. I had invested too many hours talking with Abe just to give up easily. Abe and I talked about his fall back into his old ways and what that meant for him. He said we should still talk, but he could not promise anything. So, we did. Our discussions, however, did not have the same depth as previously on both our parts. I responded to him as I heard his voice which was not as enthusiastic as it was before. Our conversations became fewer and fewer, and I knew what that meant. Abe was no longer interested in changing his behaviors because his heart was back where it once was. I could see in his eyes when we did meet, that he became totally immersed into these divisive groups on the carrier. These groups and those who shared their ideology were responsible for the graffiti and more. During some of our port visits, we were primarily confined to a small area off the ship. Of course, we had alcohol. Since alcohol usually removes inhibitions, people's actual beliefs were expressed, and this caused many issues. People began shouting racial epithets, fighting; it turned into a melee. Liberty was supposed to be a relaxing time, but a wedge was placed between whites and blacks primarily.

What added to the divide was self-segregation around the tables on liberty and on the ship, and that added to the fighting. *Self-segregation happens all the time in many places*. Self-segregation occurs because people are more comfortable with those they know, who look familiar, and have the same interests. The following example identifies one-way self-segregation happens. Using our chow time, a small group of co-workers decide to eat at the same time. They've been working together all morning, so they had a lot to talk about. They find a table with just enough chairs for them. Before long, this same group start spending all their meals together away from everyone else. Self- segregation is not wrong, but aboard an aircraft carrier it can sabotage teamwork and group dynamics. The incidents ashore made it extremely tough for everyone to get back to work on the ship. Sailors were talking about what happened, the melee, and some of those conversations created their own tense situations. Who knows how dramatic the stories of the fights became because something was added or deleted. Those involved in the fights spread the word of what happened and who said what and added their own take on things. That was their bragging rights, or so they thought. Word spread like wildfire which only created more rifts and nearly more fights. I had to assure everyone that there would be punishment for everyone involved in the melees and those who shouted racial epithets. Port visits were a challenge yet necessary for us to re-charge. Ashore we also received supplies from food to toilet paper, fuel for our fighter jets and other needed items for when we went back to sea. We were also ambassadors for the U.S during our port visits.

While on liberty I saw Abe sitting with some (later) identified racists, and I feared he was back into his old behaviors. Abe didn't get into a fight, but being with them was disappointing to me. I underestimated Abe's need to belong to a group he felt entirely comfortable around. Remember we go where we know. I understood Abe's initial dilemma about talking to me. Our total time together spanned seven months. It was unfortunate that Abe was drawn back into hate. His graffiti got worse than what he had shown me one month ago, and he totally stopped talking to me. I had no choice but to submit him for immediate discharge. Department of Defense regulation restricting anyone with racists actions or views must be separated from service. Immediate was as soon as the next day. I was sad to see him go, but I knew it was better for him and the Navy.

Looking back, Abe was uncomfortable from our first conversation. He had no idea what to expect from me and I had no idea what to expect from him especially talking about hate. Talking about race makes people uncomfortable. Combining both race and hate in a conversation can go beyond uncomfortable. But Abe and I had great conversations. Spending time with Abe watching him evolve then devolve was disheartening but I would not have missed those conversations. I learned how to approach a person who obviously has or had extremists group ties. When you are serious and have an amazing curiosity about others it is easy to talk to anyone about anything.

CHAPTER 3

Man overboard!

MAN OVERBOARD! It's Fred, I'm sure of it and I'm wringing my hands.

Fred deserved help. He was a good sailor and did his job without complaining. He was young and being on the aircraft carrier was his first time away from home. He told me he was homosexual. At that time, we still had the Don't Ask Don't Tell (D.A.D.T) policy. We couldn't ask, and homosexuals shouldn't tell their sexual preference. The regulation also stated no one could harass anyone believed to be homosexual. I told our CO and others in my chain of command about Fred because they needed to know what was happening. It was a delicate situation, but it was my job to keep things in order. Dealing with the challenges of racism, sexism, religion, I was put to the test numerous times a day. This situation had my head buzzing. A lot of moving parts. Fred's issue was that he was being harassed by his co-workers and a few supervisors. He told me some of the things being said. There were no direct statements about his sexuality but there were crude hints about it and that was against regulations. Therefore, I needed to interview some people in his department, but my schedule did not dictate when I could talk to Sailors. I scheduled interviews when it was convenient for the Sailor regardless of what time that may have been. They basically could show up anytime, and no matter what I had going on, within reason, I would take the time to hear what they had to say. Fred and all the others who needed my help deserved my best professional behavior. I always kept it strictly business keeping my bag closed.

Fred had been dealing with the harassment far too long. It was getting worse, and that's why he finally came to me. I had to do some serious thinking about how I was going to handle this. My first move was to speak to Fred's department head who was the same rank as our CO, O-6, Captain. I told the department head what Fred said had happened. At that point, I was not sure what was true, so the things Fred had said were allegations. The department head said I could do whatever I needed to get the story behind the story. *There's always a story behind the story. You must be ready to hear the other story.* Having the department head's support made my plan to interview Fred's co-workers easy. When someone breaks rules, they are defensive especially when they are called on it. I know how to ask the right questions, the correct way, and know when I should not speak and let them answer. I've listened to a Sailor for fifteento thirth minutes un-interrupted. Of course, a lot of people will tell their friends before they come talk to me what my questions are, but they get surprised. Asking each person, the same questions will more than likely get the same answers. With each Sailor, I switched it up a bit. Honestly, each person had their own unique view of the situation so depending on their role in this I had some specific questions for certain people. The co-workers thought they knew how to respond to the questions but were surprised. The truth was elusive interviewing co-workers; however, I could decipher truth from fiction. I developed that skill through years of actively listening to people tell their version.

In this department, there were only a handful of females out of over a hundred males. So, I had specific questions for the females based on their situation in the department. Fred gave me specific names of Sailors, who had harassed him. It turned out none of the females said anything negative to or about Fred. I knew who the culprits were, after a few interviews, and that made it too easy for me. Those alleged perpetrators had been in trouble quite a few times for other things. I also needed to speak to others who Fred didn't mention bothering him, because I needed their perspectives on what was happening with him. Fred was a brave young man, although his fellow Sailors were threatening to kick his ass if he ever made a move on them. These were the type of people I liked to have in my training about the Don't Ask Don't Tell policy. I used my favorite example to show some people's prejudices. I gave a common statement I'd heard about the fear of homosexuals. For instance, people would say, 'They will look at me, or they might ask me out" My statement to them was, "What makes you think that someone will find you attractive enough to look at you?" Not many people think that is humorous, but it was not intended to be. I conducted over 20 interviews including the department head. I found there was evidence of harassment and that they need to take this as their one and only warning, it needed to stop! The department head invited me to his meeting with the whole department, and he told them my findings and what was going to happen next. He stressed that all harassment would cease. Very concise and clear. I believed that everything was going to stop but I should have known better.

For about two weeks when I checked with Fred to see how things were going he told me he had no problems. Shortly after the two-week truce, Fred came to my office and said to me that things were happening again. It was not only verbal, but people had started to leave things on his rack, including horrible pictures. I saw a couple and they were disgusting. I took the pictures, and everything Fred told me was happening and went right back to the department head. He was disappointed with his Sailors, and he told them so after I did another set of interviews. Fred told me there were a few people saying things, so that made it easier to question those involved including their immediate supervisors. I wish I could chalk the harassment up to ignorance of the policy, but I conducted that training twice a year as required. I also conducted training for all Fred's co-workers, so there was no way out of what they did. No one could say they didn't know they were violating the regulation. It appeared that middle leadership was not enforcing the D.A.D.T. policy. I recommended the repeat offenders receive formal written counseling, and that would be placed in their division officer file for at least six months. If those same Sailors harassed Fred again, they would be written up, formal charges, and we would settle it that way. For leadership which allowed the harassment to continue also got formal written counseling and maintained for 90 days. Because senior leadership could not stop the harassment, they also received formal written counseling that was maintained for 90 days

To ensure things were on track with Fred, I did periodic drive-by, checking in on the work centers, and also speaking to Fred numerous times during the week. I asked his supervisors how things were going and if they needed my help. They assured me that things were under control. When we were at sea, the only day we had a slight break was Sundays. Reveille, time to start the day, on Sundays was 1200, noon, to allow people to attend church services in the morning. Reveille was 0600 the other six days. What happened next with Fred happened on a Sunday. I had the opportunity to speak to Fred quite often. He seemed great, even much better than when I first met him. He told me things were bearable, and he kept to himself as much as possible. That bothered me because he should not have to be alone to not be harassed. That's not how it worked in the Navy or for that matter in any organization. *A lack of inclusion affects productivity.* Everyone needs to be assured that if they are in trouble, they have someone to talk to whenever. Fred did not feel that anyone would help him if he were in an unsafe situation onboard. He came to see me with his concerns, but I was not in his work center to alleviate inappropriate behaviors when they happened. Once again, I expressed my concern about Fred's comments to the department head.

Fred came up with a plan to get kicked off the ship. He did not fully understand D.A.D.T. policy. Fred honestly believed that saying he was homosexual would get him an automatic discharge. He told almost everyone, including the department head, that he was homosexual. That made matters much worse. I told Fred he must stop telling people he was homosexual. Unfortunately, it was too late. His admittance about his sexual persuasion spread to way too many people and it did get more outrageous. The harassment got much worse than before. Fred was in my office at least three times a day, and I told him I would do what I could. We were both frustrated that his leaders were either ineffective or they were looking the other way. Some of the Sailors in the department said Fred is the one who is causing all the problems. They wanted him gone, and he wanted to go.

Fred's situation was not the first person to use the D.A.D.T. policy just to try to leave the Navy. I asked Fred why he thought that saying he's homosexual doesn't mean he's homosexual according to

D.A.D.T. There must be conclusive evidence a person is homosexual, i.e. seen in a kiss, picture of affection, or caught in the act. People believe they know a regulation and start being defense counsels for those who were in need. *Organizations have those same type of employees that believe they know the directives better than anyone else.* These defense counselors in the Navy are called "sea lawyers." Sea Lawyers were usually the most junior Sailors who had about one year in the Navy or is a Sailor, who had been through our disciplinary or punishment process.

They believe they know everything. All they do is create problems and false hopes. So, Fred didn't heed my words during his orientation nor the training I gave his department. I know there is an overwhelm for Sailors who have never been on a ship, much less an aircraft carrier. That was my first time on an aircraft carrier and I was overwhelmed initially. But I made it very clear that if anyone had a question about a policy or regulation they should see me. My office was very accessible and discreet. I also walked around the ship, so people could see me and ask me questions. *Phenomenal leaders get out of their office and walk around their organization. Leaders will be surprised at what he or she hears and sees.*

Obviously, Fred did not catch what I was pitching when explaining the policy. I learned we only listen to the information that pertains to us at that time. Is there ever too much training? Yes. When you train on a topic repeatedly, there comes a time that the impact of the training ceases to be positive. That's the Law of Diminishing Returns. I've suffered through that, and it was painful. Any organization should always consider the law of diminishing returns with any training no matter the subject or situation. *Training is not always the best cure for what ails an organization.*

I had to go back to my Commanding Officer with what had been happening. The CO, the JAG, (Judge Advocate General), lawyer, on the ship, and Fred's department head conferred for our next actions. Fred's department head was given time to process the Sailors who harassed Fred through the disciplinary system. I told Fred what options were available to him at that point. He could file a formal complaint against his leaders who harassed him about being homosexual. I reiterated to him that he would not be discharged because he said he was homosexual. Another part of that policy stated there had to be credible evidence determined by the Commanding Officer. The policy had very specific criteria. I ensured Fred knew about those also. This situation with Fred and his department was in about the 10th month of his time onboard. Imagine working while people make fun of you and call you names. Fred was trying to be his best self. He told me if his leaders could not only stop the harassment and discipline the instigators that he would be okay. I started the process to move him to a different berthing, a living/ sleeping area, and try to switch his work center. It is hard to move Fred to another work center because he had skills for a specific job, so he had limited options. I explained to Fred that the harassment was not going to change overnight or in three days or three weeks because he had told so many people he was homosexual. Attitudes affect behaviors, and to change attitude was not as easy as it seems. I was able to get Fred moved to a different work center. As often as I could, I checked in with him to see how his new environment was treating him. Things didn't change as quickly as Fred expected and I wanted. I could tell that he was not dealing with things so well. Something had to change soon.

Unfortunately, the change I was hoping for never happened. But change did happen. We were out to sea and it was a beautiful day without a cloud anywhere. I was enjoying a rare slow day. Fred stopped by my office, and I could see that he was feeling down. I asked him how things were going, and he said it pretty much sucked. He told me he was in his berthing, and some co-workers started calling him names and making fun of him. I asked Fred specifically what they said. He stated that they called him a 'homo,' 'freak,' 'fag,' 'fudge packer', and more. I was amazed at their ignorance, cruelty, arrogance, and willingness to receive punishment by using prohibited words. What made me totally incensed was the way Fred's supervisors basically got away with doing nothing to maintain any professionalism and setting an awful leadership example. Doing nothing is doing the wrong something every time. He said they also told him not to say anything or else they would beat his ass. Fred was fighting back tears as he spoke. After Fred had finished speaking, some tears did flow. I gave him a minute to compose himself then asked him if he really felt threatened by his co-workers. He shook his head no. I'm not sure I believed him, but he had to tell me if going back to his berthing was a threatening thought. I had never seen him so upset. Fred needed a break from all the drama. I let him stay in my office as long as he wanted. I didn't have any good remedies for him, so I had to ask him again to be a little more patient. Although he was in my office for around 30 minutes, he had only talked for about ten minutes. There was one thing Fred never did was to give me specific names of those who were giving him such a bad time. That made the change of attitudes and behaviors much harder. I did ask the leadership if they knew and I only got a couple of names. Everyone in that department knew who was saying things. Fred was actually protecting those who were tormenting him, or he was scared they would beat his ass. He had a genuinely very kind soul. I really felt for him and just couldn't come up with anything to make his Navy experience more rewarding and enjoyable. But my feelings had nothing to do with what should be done about Fred and his woes.

On that same beautiful day, Fred said he was okay and finally left my office. I immediately called his department head and told him about Fred's visit. I was adamant that people should be held accountable for what they do and say. That included his upper management who were the actual culprits. As leaders, they were not there to make friends but to lead. That is the same for any organization. *Referent Leadership is based on how well a person is liked giving him or her options to get   work done.* On a carrier, there was a different urgency because when launching aircraft, one can't worry about upsetting a friend when things needed to get done. I've seen friendship derail workplace productivity and sometimes drive employees out of an organization.

Back to Fred. It is still a beautiful day. It is warm, the sun is bright, we were launching and recovering aircraft. The water is so blue and clean, and it smells fresh. I thought to myself another fantastic day. Not soon after Fred had left my office, I hear one whistle, two, three and finally four. That was how everyone was alerted that there is a man overboard. The announcement on the 1MC, shipboard announcement system, "man overboard, man overboard port side. Move up and forward on the port side down and aft on the starboard side." At that moment, Sailors are moving quickly through the passageways to get to their mustering station. It is controlled chaos. We only had a few minutes to muster, so we knew who was missing and probably overboard. When I heard the first whistle, it caught my attention. As the second, third, and fourth, whistle sounded I began to panic. I didn't know what a panic attack was until then. I rushed to my mustering station and told my department head I had to go to talk to the Executive Officer, XO, who was responsible for launching our recovery boat, launching a helicopter and getting the final muster to determine who was in the water. As I ran, I felt my heart in my throat beating faster and faster. I was dizzy, and I stopped to walk for a while. I started running again because I felt a sense of urgency to get to the XO.

I couldn't think straight, but I knew where I needed to be, with the XO. I was sweating, and it was rolling down my face. What seemed like hours was only a couple of minutes, and I finally got to the XO. He was surprised to see me there, but he could tell something was wrong. I can hear my voice now trembling and needing to tell him what I knew. I said, "I know who is in the water. It is Fred. He just left my office. It is Fred." I started pacing and listening for reports from either the helicopter or rescue boat. The XO was trying to calm me and reassure me that it would all be okay. My heart was coming out of my chest. I was pacing. What had I said to Fred to make him jump off the ship? Had I driven him to jump? I'm pacing. How long has it been? I remember praying, please don't let him die. I said that prayer over and over. *Why is it taking so long? It has been five minutes.* My fingers were hurting, but I didn't know why until I realized I had been wringing my hands. My two friends found me and asked me what was going on. It's now nine minutes into recovery and no word. I told them, and they started reassuring me that Fred would be fine. This was my fault. I should have seen this coming that day. I was still pacing and praying. My friends tried to calm me down, but I was too keyed up. I kept going over what just happened a few minutes ago in my office. Eleven minutes and nothing. I didn't know what I said or should have said. We are still waiting for word about his status. Suddenly the radio crackled, and I stopped. Fourteen minutes went by and nothing. I was pacing and praying. Finally, I heard him say that it was a safe recovery, and Fred was fine. I fell to my knees to thank God Fred was okay. I was still shaking, and my friends took me to sit down. My respirations started slowing down. I'm not okay, but I'm better. Now I'm thinking what I should say to Fred now.

After we had recovered the small boat and helicopter, other things began. The legal process started immediately and what usually took a couple of days only took about ten minutes. Fred was about to get his wish. The punishment for jumping overboard was a discharge. As part of my job I went to all the disciplinary and legal procedures. All reported to the signal bridge for Captain's Mast. The view was spectacular. Fred had to get checked out by our medical officer. He was okay. They bring Fred in, and he is still in the clothes he jumped overboard in and the water was dripping off him everywhere. All ship jumpers went through this same process the same way wet clothes and all. I noticed that Fred was shaking, and I didn't know if he was cold, scared, or both. Fred apologized to the CO for putting his fellow Sailors at risk saving him. He thanked me for helping him and listening to him when he needed to talk. This CO's mast, punishment, was almost record time. It only took about five minutes to go through the mast. An average mast was about fifteen minutes depending on the number of witnesses. The Commanding Officer is never happy when someone jumps off the ship. It is very dangerous when we launch the boat off the side of a moving ship. Additionally, launching anything off a moving aircraft carrier is hazardous to the crew and the Sailors who work on the flight deck. There are many ways this could have turned out. Fortunately, everyone was okay and we all got what we wanted.

What happened to Fred was unfortunate and extremely unprofessional. Not to mention he finally showed his frustration and disappointment with the Navy. This should have never happened, and I needed to ensure it didn't happen again. This whole situation was not fair to Fred. He presented me with some serious issues with challenging circumstances. It stretched me, and now I have more skills and am highly effective when dealing with extremely personal issues. But things are about to get very exciting at a whole new level in a totally different way.

CHAPTER 4

I would not save you!

I HAD SPOKEN WITH STEFFAN for 2.5 hours, and he still would let me burn in a fire.

Steffan was new to the Navy; he'd been in for about eight months.

He was nineteen years old. He's assigned to the department that "fights" the ship. That means if there is a flood, fire, or weapon issue, etc. these Sailors are specifically trained for those situations. They are our first responders.

Steffan was a brilliant young man. He was from upstate Minnesota, and he said that he was adopted. Steffan was a hardcore racist. I don't use the word racist lightly because it is a harsh word. There should be substantial evidence before calling someone racist. That's a stigma that's hard to shed. Due diligence is required when dealing with an alleged racist. *The word racist is powerful and accuses that person of hating others that don't look like him or her.* Steffan was a racist.

A little more background on Steffan. He told me he was adopted, at ten years old, and his adoptive parents were great. He didn't say if his parents were aware if his participation in hate groups. I asked him if his parents believed the same derogatory thoughts he did. Steffan said no, that he was recruited by a hate group, and he discovered he loved their doctrine, enjoyed the planned activities, believed in violence against African-Americans, and much more. He was proud being in an extremist group. Steffan joined his first extremist group at the age of seven. He was already in a hate group by the time he was adopted. That is not uncommon for very young people to join a group, so they feel wanted and get the love some of them are craving. They have activities like parties, outings, concerts, and much more. I've seen a KKK meeting on video, and infants were wearing a KKK hood ensuring young children are socialized into hate thinking from day one.

With all Steffan told me I was surprised he joined the Navy. He said his parents were surprised too. Apparently, he was socialized into his hate group which made it hard to work with those who were different from him as far as race and ethnicity. Steffan didn't have much or any interaction with African-Americans or Latinos/Hispanics while growing up, so his hate started with someone else's feelings toward minorities. A lot of extremist group members have limited interactions with those they hate, and they believe what everyone else is telling them. The saying 'ignorance is bliss.' is an accurate description of hate groups' thinking.

What I find amazing is how Steffan made it through boot camp. There are very close quarters, and teamwork is necessary for everyone to complete boot camp. He told me that he stayed as far away from African-Americans as possible. I admit that would be very hard to do but not impossible. Steffan also had to go to school for his specialty, and it would have been even harder there to stay away from African- Americans because of the type of training. Firefighting and lifesaving are only two of the skills Steffan had to learn in the training; these skills require close quarters.

Now Steffan is on the carrier straight out of his specialty school. He stated he was excited about being on his first ship and looked forward to port visits. During my onboarding training, he didn't say anything when I talked about the extremist activity on the ship. Of course, I didn't expect him to shout out he was a racist. I showed tattoos, graffiti, and spoke with a stern voice so everyone knew that there were consequences to placing their hate on display. I did a ton of research on hate groups and hate symbols. I learned and taught about hate and various tattoos I'd seen on the ship's bulkheads (walls) and on Sailors' bodies. Here are a few of the tattoos and graffiti: **100%** - meaning the person is 100% White; 14 – the 14 words: We must secure the existence of our society and the future for white children.

 These are Doc Marten boots, and red or white shoelaces shows they are racist skinheads; **RAHOWA** – racial holy war. There are some hate groups symbols that are stolen symbols with a different meaning.

 The swastika is the oldest cross in the world and was taken from various religions. The original is 4 L's – Love, Light, Luck, and Life. Anti-Defamation League (ADL) has much more information.

Steffan volunteered he had five tattoos which I could not see unless he took off his shirt. He had all these tattoos before entering the Navy. The Navy adopted regulations that stated tattoos could not be seen. The Navy started removing tattoos for Sailors, and I heard it was painful. I didn't see Steffan's tattoos until he came to my office for the "chat." I called it a chat because it was not counseling, but it was a serious conversation. Chat takes the sting out of an interview. That's what I used when I thought things could get crazy. Steffan was on the carrier for about eight months without any incidents. However, during one of our port visits his true colors came out. Steffan was sitting with a group of Caucasian guys, some I knew, and they had been drinking for about four hours, and it was sunny and extremely hot. Alcohol and heat are not a good combo. It started simply enough somebody said something or bumped into someone I'm not sure. But what comes next was eye opening.

A flurry of nigger, wetback, bitch, white boy broke through the noise of the DJ and general party fun. When words like that are said, Sailors had to come to me for the chat. Steffan knew who I was because he went through my onboarding training and I used pictures of graffiti. Some Sailors couldn't believe the amount of graffiti or the harshness and the rest just absorbed it in. Here is some of the graffiti I saw; "Niggers smell like sh*t because they don't take showers. They are nasty." Another "We should kill all the niggers." There was even a drawing of a noose with a 'nigger' hanging from it like the game hangman. The letters spelled nigger. There was very little graffiti about Caucasians and it was not nearly as violent. The one I remember was found in a passageway, and it stated, "White people are the devil", and there was a picture of a 'white guy' with devil ears holding a pitch fork and had a long tail. There were a few Sailors concerned about being at sea with people who believed those words and drawings. I talked to those Sailors to assure them there was nothing to worry about. They thought their safety was at risk, but I reassured everyone that these Sailors were the minority of individuals, and we keep a tight watch on that activity. Steffan knew he had done something wrong, in the Navy's eyes, but he had no idea he was going to visit me. We left port and I prepared for the chats about the chaos that occurred. Preparing for chats like these took me out of my comfort zone, yet I was and needed to be calm. I know the Sailors I talk to will be out of their comfort zone as well. I was intrigued how Steffan made it through boot camp and his specialty school with no incident like this.

Our conversation moved from his background to the day of the melee. My office was long but not very wide, so the utilizable space was tiny, even though there were two of us who worked in there. I had only about 3 feet of distance from the Sailors who came to see me. When Sailors first saw my office, they were surprised at the place we would be having our chat. Steffan was my first conversation with a real racist, and my friends and office mate asked if I wanted one of them in the office just in case. I told them that wouldn't work. I was a bit nervous and not only because Steffan was a racist, but I needed to get as much information out of him I possibly could. Steffan was a few minutes early, and that was good because I was ready to get started, I'm not sure about him. My desk was on a rise, so initially I was always above everyone. When Steffan walked into my office, I was sitting at my desk to make a silent statement. I needed him to know that I was in charge of this chat, and I had no fear of him. He had a seat, and my officemate asked me one more time if I wanted him to stay, and I told him no and off he went. I started the conversation by asking him background questions. Still sitting in my chair, I asked Steffan if he knew why he was there and his initial answer was no. That's when I sat on the rise for my chair and desk, so I was only about a foot away from him. I had tried to lighten the mood at the beginning, so he got used to answering my questions. But now it is time to get real. I asked Steffan what had triggered his flurry of racial epithets. He said there was too much that he had overlooked, and he was tired of not being himself. He told me that he had been faking getting along with African-Americans and the other minorities. I noticed he was getting a little ticked off, and that's what I wanted at that time of the chat. If he was getting angry, then he will lose his inhibitions and say what he means. I asked him to tell me what he meant by overlooking things. One of his examples was standing in the chow, meal line. It was crowded, people were standing close, so others could pass by them. It was always crowded there because the passageway was not too wide, so Sailors were usually so close they accidently touched each other.

Steffan said he happened to be between two African-American Sailors, and he felt trapped. He decided to move out of line and wait until there was a spot with a few Caucasians. He also stated that other times throughout the workday, seven days a week, he was more concerned that he could not avoid African-Americans while doing his work; his supervisors considered his work outcomes effective, so it did not initially effect his work. However, there were times when Steffan had no focus on his responsibilities or his job; but he was expected to be in the game all the time because that was the only way the ship would survive any disaster. Based on what he told me he had lapses of judgment in his work. But he was adamant that his work was never negatively affected. His eye contact was initially a hard stare. His other body language was rather closed, leaning away from me, reinforcing his stare, showing me, he was not interested in what I was saying. Steffan was not interested in the whole process we were going through.

Steffan stated that he mainly despised African-Americans. Other minorities were tolerable sometimes but African-Americans never. He made direct eye contact with me when he made that statement. I was looking right back at him, without being phased by what he just said. It was difficult for me to maintain my composure, but I didn't give him the satisfaction of getting upset or showing fear. I would have been totally unprofessional and that was and is not me. Steffan continued with the typical rhetoric; African-Americans are dirty, lazy, loud, rude, either on drugs or selling drugs or both, and he went on for about another minute and as he did I shook my head to show I was really listening to him. Showing interest in what he was saying changed his body language a little as in Steffan was willing to listen but not buying what I was selling. I asked him why he said all those derogatory things about African-Americans because he spent no time with them? He told me he knew these things because they were true; he learned all this from his hate group.

Steffan knew I wanted to see his tattoos, so he asked me if I wanted to see them now. He took off his shirt and t-shirt and then I saw them. He had a large swastika on his right shoulder, a Celtic Cross, 88, 100%, and a skull inside the type of army hat the Germans wore. Steffan elaborated about each tattoo. All his tattoos were large and easy to read. He did have a couple I didn't recognize, and he said those he made up himself. I could tell he was very proud of his tattoos. I thought that was good since they are nearly permanent. I believe he thought that by showing me his tattoos was a way for him to feel he was in control of our chat. Our power to control the conversation changed frequently. His tattoos were a big symbol of who he was as a person. The only thing about his tattoos is that a few others will see them and might be curious. Steffan will tell anyone about his tattoos and why he has them. That scenario could create problems for me and others.

Steffan sat back down. I asked him where he learned all these things about African-Americans. He told me that his extremist group proved everything he said and more. He said the first time he really had to interact with African-Americans was in boot camp. I asked him to pick an African-American leader on this ship and describe her from his limited contact with her. He chose a Master Chief Petty Officer, enlisted E-9 most senior rank for enlisted Sailors, I knew who he was talking about because she was the only African-American female E-9 and we were friends. He said she was professional, intelligent, friendly personality, sense of humor, and he could tell she loved the Navy. I asked him why he didn't say she was lazy or rude. The more questions I asked, Steffan was getting a bit agitated, moving side to side on his chair and deep sighs. He didn't have an answer to my question about the Master Chief. What an opening he gave me. I asked if he thought the Master Chief was an exception to his rule about African-Americans. Again, he had no answer. I answered for him saying she must be different. Notice this "exception" to the rule is a way to justify using a stereotype. We had been talking for about an hour, and I was just getting started. Steffan knew about recruiting for hate groups. I was pretty sure he wouldn't tell me any names or specifics about his fellow racists, but I had to try. I moved closer to him a couple of inches. I asked him if he was recruiting Sailors to some unnamed hate group he belongs to or was the leader. He was surprised at my question. He was silent for a bit, and I thought he was not going to answer me. However, Steffan said, " Do you think I'm going to tell you anything like that, no way." I expected that answer but had to ask just in case he was feeling generous. He looked at me with a bit of anger that I would ask him such a thing. Finally, I got some real emotion from him, and that's what I wanted.

I moved a bit closer, and I could see he was getting real uncomfortable. My intention was to keep his emotions high and genuine. I turned the conversation around and asked him what kind of music he liked. He looked at me and said heavy metal and alternative rock. I asked if he liked Tool or Godsmack. Steffan looked puzzled. Then I asked if he liked Korn. He suddenly started laughing and asked if I actually listened to those groups. I told him not only do I listen to them I've seen them in concert. I asked him why he was laughing and if he thought I was too old to listen to groups like that. He smirked and said I didn't know African-Americans listened to music like that. I went further and told him that an African-American got me interested in heavy metal/alternative rock music. I bet him he would be surprised at other things I liked or did. I asked Steffan what else he likes, and he chose his favorite outdoor activity which was hunting. I added no racist rallies or anything like that. He and I both laughed. We continued to talk about things we liked or disliked. For about two minutes he forgot why he hated someone who looked like me. He couldn't believe what we both liked. I asked him what he learned from this experience. He started off by saying, I still don't like African-Americans. The exchange we just had meant nothing. Steffan added that just because we like some of the same things does not make us friends. I agreed. He said it was just weird talking about our mutual likes. Again, I agreed. Some people thought I was crazy when I told them about this part of my chat. But when two or more diverse people discover some common ground that must be explored. That is the basis of teamwork in a diverse environment, healthy curiosity.

I didn't lose sight of why Steffan and I were talking. I knew I couldn't change his beliefs or behaviors around minorities in this short period of time, so that was not one of my purposes. I strived to give him a different perspective of African-Americans. The importance of changing perspectives is rarely if ever discussed when talking race. *Changing attitudes, beliefs, or lasting behavior change will cause frustration.*

During conversations about race to a racist, I had to keep focused on the behavior and not the person. Steffan judged a person by the color of their skin. *Now is a good time to bring more truth.* Some African-Americans are just as racist as Caucasians. Using the theory of racism, it is possible for any race to be racist. The theory – a belief that a race has specific characteristics or qualities that distinguish it as inferior or superior to another race. There is no excuse for any race to hate another because we all have things in common, and our differences keep life spicy. Imagine this...the entire world is filled with only people like you. Everyone looks like you, talks like you, eats like you and works like you, on and on. Never anything new, always the same faces, the same good things, and all a person's shortcomings can never be escaped. I'm sure you would be ready for something new and fast. It's like eating steak for breakfast, lunch, and dinner and snacks if needed. Diversity makes life exciting. How do conversations about race start? I have an excellent way to do that. Questions. *Not just any questions, but safe ones that will create dialogue.* I'll cover more about the questions in Chapter 10. Here are a few of the queries I use to help people start talking to someone, not like them. Here are three you should use. What is your favorite food? Which weather season do you prefer? Where do you go to get some alone time? As you see the questions are not confrontational. Initially I was a bit nervous talking with Steffan, but I stayed on track thinking about how I might plant one good thought in Steffan's head. Finding some common ground is an excellent way to plant a good seed.

Those are the type questions I asked Steffan. And we got past the African-American/Caucasian thing. For a moment, Steffan and I were best friends, but it was very short period of time, only minutes. Especially when we were talking about musical groups we like. I believe racists should be given a chance to take a step in a positive direction. If not, then how can they try to change? I believe racists can shed some of their beliefs by changing their perspectives. This reminds me of the movie American History X made in 1998 starring Edward Norton. I highly recommend it. There are racists using bad language, but the movie is worth every dollar. I will be using some quotes from this film because they fit very well. The movie plot is a former neo-Nazi skinhead tries to prevent his younger brother from going down the same wrong path that he did. Edward Norton's character, Derek, killed a black kid in front of his brother. His brother thought that was awesome. While in prison, Derek befriends an African-American man, so Derek changes his beliefs and attitudes about African-Americans. There is one quote, I'll be using quite a bit. Derek's (Edward Norton), younger brother Danny, Edward Furlong said, *"Well, my conclusion is: Hate is baggage. Life's too short to be pissed off all the time. It's just not worth it."*

Bringing in the movie is to show how racists can change even if it is a movie, so we must try. The final part of my chat with Steffan is how I started the chapter. As I closed the chat I asked one last question. Steffan's job was to save the ship in a casualty situation and to save a person in imminent danger if he could. So, I asked him if he would save me if I was unconscious in a burning room and he could get to me safely.

Steffan looked me straight in the eyes and said "no." With that, I wished him well in civilian life.

Steffan could not pick and choose who he would save in an emergency. If he did, he would be a danger to everyone on the ship. At least he was honest. After spending time with Steffan I was so prepared to talk to another racist. And of course, I did.

CHAPTER 5

Get Your Paper Right Here

I NEVER READ THE WASHINGTON POST (WP) until 2000. In 2000, I was stationed at the Washington Navy Yard, Washington, D.C., as the Equal Opportunity Advisor/Diversity Officer (EOA/DO).

One of my responsibilities was to ensure there was an equitable work environment in each organization. I was asked to go to the Navy's premier dental school. They were graduating some of the top dentist in the Navy, and in the U.S. Dentists would graduate in the specialty of maxillofacial prosthetics which can fix or replace parts of the face, ears and teeth. These students were very talented. The chain of command was worried that the school environment was a bit hostile and maybe unfair. I was tasked to assess the work environment and based on the feedback to the school's Captain(CO) and my boss make recommendations if an investigation was needed. I deemed an investigation was necessary. I had to gather all my confidence because the instructors were all O-6, Captains, and I was an E-7, Chief Petty Officer, (refer to Military Ranks Chapter 1) and I knew those Captains would question both my authority and skills to do this investigation. Although there was a substantial difference in our paygrades I was more than qualified to conduct this investigation. I prepared questions for each person who was a student, instructor, and worked there as support staff. I conducted 50 interviews, day and night, in less than a month and presented my findings. But it was not as simple as I just stated above.

All this started with a student being dropped from the dental school for failure to meet performance standards. But it wasn't just a student; it was an African-American male, Oscar, and all the instructors, and the CO, are Caucasians. Oscar did not agree with his dismissal because he believed it was based on him being an African-American. Oscar's next step should have been to file a formal complaint against the Commander through me. However, he decided to go to the Washington Post(WP) instead of coming to us, next in his chain of command, as stated in the policy. When we saw the article in the WP, we had to move fast to find Oscar and ask him what's going on. I did catch up with Oscar and we speak about the article in the Washington Post. I told him what he should have done, but he didn't know how upset we were. I went over the policy with Oscar. I helped him complete the complaint that he needed to although I was assigned to do the investigation. That's the duality of my job as EOA/DO.

I need to highlight the difference in my rank compared to the ranks of some of those I interviewed. Interviews with my seniors would be like a middle manager going straight to the CEO and questioning her about her behavior. But I knew what I was doing so I didn't think about the rank difference. Some of those Captains, doctors, were a little ticked off because they didn't think I should be conducting the investigation nor asking them questions. That's the beauty of having trained specialists because rank had nothing to do with my knowledge, skills, abilities, and talents to carry out the investigation.

As I got into interviews, that's when I heard some disturbing things. There were only seven students in Oscar's class.   Very few students graduate because of the intensity of the school and profession. The class was rather diverse for its size. There was one African-American male, one Indian male, one Asian male, and four Caucasian males, and one Caucasian female. I was surprised at what the minority students told me; this is where it got disturbing. First, all the instructors treated them the same except for the female. She received extra help and was allowed additional time to complete her work. The instructors are dentists who were very experienced in what they were teaching. The students are dentists also, so she should have some level of expertise in a few things they were doing.

Second, according to the students, some of the instructors made jokes about students' ethnicity. Here's an example, the day before Oscar was dismissed from the school the Indian male was not at a meeting. The instructor pointed out he missed the meeting and the instructor said it had something to do with his ethnicity and country of origin.

Next, is what happens nearly everywhere, unfortunately. A student said that inappropriate and insensitive comments were made about Catholics, Italians, Polish, and more. Oscar added that no one race, ethnicity or religion was singled out, it was an even dose of inappropriate comments. He said instructors made all the comments and they said something derogatory about everyone and that was okay. Oh yeah, let's not forget jokes. If it is a joke, it is okay to say derogatory things. Too many people believe that if there is laughter there's nothing wrong. Even more, students stated that the instructors used derogatory comments to each other. Inappropriate comments are inappropriate comments regardless of who says it to whom. Wrong is wrong even if everyone agrees. Another student said he was uncomfortable in the school and that some days he just wanted to leave. All this because of "jokes" that anyone could be the recipient of and the lack of respect for the students.

Finally, the students were already incredibly talented, and that's the reason they were at this prestigious school. They graduate as some of the top dentists in the U.S. That was enough motivation to keep students silent when the instructors made inappropriate comments. No one wanted extra attention because the next joke may be about him or her. The school was challenging enough without adding insults but some of the instructors seemed oblivious to the effect they had on their students. The instructors were so arrogant and thought they were untouchable and could do whatever they want. There were never any jokes told the whole month I was there so obviously the instructors could refrain from their jokes.

Oscar made the same comments as the other students. He stated that no one dared to say something to the instructors about their comments, or they would suffer consequences. Those consequences are called reprisal. The Navy has rules about reprisal, but they just didn't want to take the risk. All the minority students agreed that if they complained the instructors would take some adverse action. Oscar, as well as the other minorities, said they felt intimidated and feared to go above the instructors about their poor work environment. There are five types of power and they are: legitimate, coercive, referent, reward and expert. The instructors had legitimate, reward, and expert power and they showed it as a badge.

As far as Oscar's interview it took three days. Each day was at least four to five hours, no kidding. I didn't want him to feel rushed through his story and I needed his entire story. I also required as much information as possible from him, so I'd know who to re-interview or discover someone else I needed to interview and who knew what. When we specifically talked about his dismissal situation, Oscar felt relieved that his story would be told. He had never had the chance to tell his whole story to anyone in the Navy. After we got through some easy relaxing questions I got into his real issues. First, I wanted to know how he evaluated his performance at school. That one question allowed Oscar to speak non-stop for about three hours. It was tough for me to just sit and listen because I wanted to ask questions while Oscar's mind was fresh in a situation. I took extensive notes, so I could clarify some things he said with my own questions. Oscar had never been interviewed before ours, although he did go over his story with his attorney. His attorney actually wanted to meet me, so we had a short conversation. After six hours I ended the interview, and he came back the following day. Again, I allowed him to talk without interruption for about four hours. But now I had to start asking the hard questions. Oscar needed to tell and show me what actions he considered discriminatory, so I could develop thorough interview questions.

Oscar said that he was just as proficient in his work or even better than a couple of the students, until he had a major life event happen—his father died. The school allowed him to go home and paused his school requirements. Oscar believed his father's death affected him more than he realized. He said he tried to catch up on the work he had left and became overwhelmed and didn't know who to talk to about his issues. He attempted to do what he could, but that was not good enough. Oscar's work, according to Oscar, did fall short of the expectations. I had documentation from his instructors about his performance. Additionally, I had all the other interview summaries about how he did in school. The majority of all the data I reviewed characterized Oscar's performance as mediocre or even worse than that. He did admit that his performance slipped, but it was no worse than any other student. Of course, there are three sides to every story: the school, Oscar's, and somewhere in the middle the truth.

It's important to know what was in the Washington Post because that's what started this and I haven't given it to you yet. Remember my name was not listed but nearly everyone who worked in the Navy Yard knew me. One of my friends contacted me and said he saw my "name" in the WP. I saw it and was surprised. We thought it was better for me not to be identified, and I totally agreed. His attorney used my position's responsibilities and my job very specifically in his interview with the WP. I knew he would refer to me again after my first step in this process and he did. Of course, the attorney used my job title when I finished the discrimination portion of my investigation. I didn't need fame. Oscar told his story and accused the instructors of discrimination because he was dismissed from the school. He had one instructor on his side. That instructor was interviewed by the WP journalist. Joe, we'll call him, characterized one meeting as a "lynching" of Oscar. Unfortunately, Oscar wanted his situation told outside the Navy. Maybe he thought that would ensure he was treated fairly by everyone involved. We asked Oscar, after we told him what was going to happen, to please stop the newspaper articles. Did that happen? No. There were three more articles in the WP. I told him I could not do my investigation effectively if he kept providing all the details of his case so anyone could read it. I can't trust who I interview because I don't know if they were telling me their actual story or repeating what they read in the newspaper. I needed him to stop talking to the Washington Post or I couldn't complete my investigation. Of course, Oscar had the right to talk to the journalist, but it made the whole process more difficult and unreliable. Once I told him, that stopped his articles.

Joe was what I call a wild card in this investigation. As one of his instructors, Joe, gave a statement, unlike all the other instructors. He said during an instructor meeting one of them said 'Listen, the bottom line is, do we really want his kind to be in our specialty?' In this same meeting, Joe stated the other doctors voted to dismiss Oscar, and he had to go along with the other doctors. Joe said that the other instructors distorted why he voted for dismissal the same way they did. Joe added that he considered that meeting to be more or less a lynching. According to Joe, the other instructors stated that Oscar was in the cross hairs. He believed that Oscar was set-up and didn't have a chance to remain in school. The next fact is unfortunate. Joe said, and I verified, that no African-American officer has ever completed the residency program. There was one other African-American male resident, I interviewed who said he decided to resign on his own. He did not feel there was any direct discrimination. There was no comment about any indirect discrimination. The phone call was rather cryptic, and it didn't really add any value to the investigation.

There were way too many assumptions made in this school setting. The most common assumptions were that when an instructor made derogatory statements saying, 'that was a joke' meant no one could take offense. A work environment seething with intimidation and fear will ultimately have poor results. And just because a work environment produces doesn't mean all is well, and that things couldn't be better. Good leaders should know that not everyone will speak up when they believe something is wrong. Good leaders also ensure their work environment fosters respect. Silence is consent and gives those who say offensive things permission to continue.

To complete this complaint, I drew a few conclusions based on the facts I had gathered. Instructors confused poor performance with lack of talent by a student. The instructors could never see how wrong some of their behaviors were towards their students. Another conclusion was that the Commander was out of touch with his command. Things should not have gotten so bad that a student had to go to the Washington Post to get his grievance heard. I also concluded the evidence supported a finding that the instructors used unprofessional and disparaging remarks about Oscar and other students. However, I could not find that Oscar's dismissal was racially motivated. I did conclude that the circumstances surrounding Oscar's dismissal were questionable as to the appropriateness of his removal. Therefore, my boss ordered that Oscar be reinstated immediately. And that happened as soon as reasonably possible. There were some unhappy, actually, pissed off, instructors.

However, my job was not complete. I periodically monitored Oscar's work environment to ensure he did not suffer any reprisals. I ensured all the instructors and the commander knew I would be watching. What impact did my visits have on the instructors? They would never admit it, but their levity was tempered which students and instructors hated. Students hated the instructors to be so serious all the time. Helping the instructors, I talked to them and told them they could still have fun just not as someone else's expense. The monitoring was also useful to ensure changes were made based on my findings and recommendations. Additionally, I had a very frank conversation with Oscar before he was reinstated. I made sure he knew that I would be watching for reprisals, and he should contact me immediately if he believed that was happening. Most importantly I told him that this was his last chance to show everyone that he belonged in that school. This was a high-stakes move for Oscar and the school. Unfortunately, Oscar only lasted six months, and he was dismissed again for his poor performance. No WP this time. He didn't even tell me. I heard it from someone else. I'm sure he was disappointed. I'm sure the school felt vindicated.

All was not lost. After one year I interviewed the minority students to gauge the change in the school. I was very pleased to learn that the derogatory comments had ceased. As I walked around the entire school and made some quick impromptu interviews, it was evident that professionalism had been restored. Professionalism breeds so many positives in an organization, and that is seen and heard. Respect is earned and given. The investigation also created open communications, so the students felt less pressure and were free to be themselves. Allowing students to speak freely and anonymously if possible was necessary. The students said that freedom enabled them to perform at higher levels and give their best selves.

There are many outtakes from this entire situation. Ensure your employees know and understand policies such as sexual harassment, EEOC information, and reprisal. Another outtake is CEOs must keep in touch with his or her work environment. He or she can do this by taking the time to walk around talk to employees, students, managers, instructors and more. The CEO must also keep tabs on his or her senior executives with impromptu meetings. The Senior executives should monitor managers and supervisors' behaviors by face to face meetings every other month. Assess work environment climate. One way to alleviate fear and intimidation is by being open and having brown bag luncheons will work. Employees need to see that the supervisors, managers, and CEO are approachable.

Some people yell from the mountain top and others whisper. Oscar and Joe decided to yell. In a good work environment when there are issues they are handled within the organization. Great work environments can almost sense when something is wrong, and they take action immediately. A pro-active organization communications flow, people produce at an extremely high level, and any other positives an organization can achieve. Take a risk on people .and they can surprise you.

I was as surprised as the young Sailor who burst into my office.

CHAPTER 6

Imagine His Surprise

"I WON'T WORK FOR NIGGERS."

That's how I met Sam. He barged right into my office without knocking nor seeing me initially. Sam didn't know who he was there to talk to, but I finally caught his eyes. My office mate was Caucasian. I know he wanted it to be her. If I could have taken a picture I most definitely would. I'll try to describe it the best I can.

My door flew open, and I saw Sam, his face was red, he was out of breath, and he was sweating. He was young and Caucasian. He had blonde hair and blue eyes. The perfect Aryan according to Adolf Hitler. His uniform was very disheveled, and he could hardly speak. However, he had just enough air to tell me why he was there. I knew he was coming to my office because his supervisor called me. When Sam turned to look at me, his mouth fell open, and suddenly he stopped right at the open door. He almost looked like a statue. I told him to come on in and have a seat. He did, but his eyes were moving side to side, I could tell he was thinking. Sam was uncomfortable.

I asked him why he came to my office without knocking on the door. Rather softly he answered, not as loud as when he first burst into my office, so I really couldn't understand what he was saying. I asked him to repeat his answer. He told me why he was sent there. I could see he didn't know what to expect from me.

He came in and sat down. I told Sam that in the Navy we don't use derogatory language. He said sorry without looking at me. I told Sam he had to obey lawful orders even if they are from an African-American. If Sailors didn't follow lawful orders, then nothing would be accomplished and there would be anarchy.

We begin. Sam was 18 years old. Sam and Steffan said nigger around me without a blink. So, our conversations were very open and honest. I told all three of them, Steffan and Abe, that the only way our chats would be successful was if we could speak freely. I could correct them when needed. Everyone agreed. My office mate left before I started talking to Sam because she was a bit uncomfortable. I needed the office to myself with Sam. By this time, I am comfortable talking to racists alone. I started out asking Sam to tell me about himself. He grew up in a small town in Texas. I told him I grew up in a small town in Kentucky.

I asked if there were any African-Americans in his town and he said there were only Caucasians. That explained why he was not excited about taking orders from African-American Sailors. Sam was socialized by that whole town figuratively speaking. They gave him permission to use derogatory terms because there was no one there saying those words were wrong. I asked him how he made it through boot camp. Sam said he kept away from minorities when possible. Then I asked him why he joined the Navy knowing there are African-Americans. He didn't think about it. He said when he got to boot camp he realized this wouldn't be easy.

So now Sam is on this aircraft carrier with a lot of African-American Sailors with nowhere to go. He felt lost and reverted to what he knew. African-Americans are giving him orders about what to do surely shocked his beliefs, truths, and values. His reaction was not unlike anyone else who is confronted by something incongruent with what they know. Sam thought he knew everything and didn't want to hear anything about anyone. I asked him what he knew about African- Americans since he just came in contact with us. His reply was almost the same as Abe and Steffan. Sam told me with confidence that African-Americans are lazy, loud, conceited, stupid, thieves, play rap music too loud, they use drugs, and physically fight anyone including themselves. I asked him how he learned all these things without being in contact with African-Americans. Sam said his family and friends told him, the movies and the news helped affirm what he had learned. That is classic deliberate socialization. Remember from Chapter 1 the factors that impact socialization? The 24-hour news cycle reinforces that African-Americans are criminals because most times African-Americans are on the news it is usually something criminal. There is data that supports the news especially when the data is skewed because African-American neighborhoods are patrolled more and tighter than other communities. That allows Caucasians to keep perpetuating the lies that fit their reality. Yes, I called them lies because what Abe, Steffan, and Sam believed was not only true about African-Americans.

Although the average person has no idea about crime stats some of them not reported are very telling. If we don't have the right information, then our conclusions or beliefs about any race or ethnicity are skewed. We must be vigilant about how and what neighborhoods are policed because that will make biased statistics. The 24-hour news cycle doesn't always present all sides of an issue. Based on certain data Sam had a right to think negatively and easily hate African-Americans.

Sam reminded me of Danny in the movie American History X first mentioned in Chapter 4. Derek Vineyard played by Edward Norton was a hardcore racist, he killed a young African-American kid by slamming his head on the concrete curb outside his house. It took a Significant Emotional Event (SEE) to change Derek's view of minorities. SEEs don't happen that often but they are powerful because they will change your life one way or another. That happened to Derek in prison. His work and cell mate were an African-American and they eventually became friends after many altercations. Although, Derek's SEE took some time, just being around his cell mate 24/7 changed Derek's opinion about African-Americans. Derek did not want his younger brother Danny to follow in his footsteps as a racist, but it was too late. Danny had been socialized by Derek's ex-hate group. Danny is murdered before he graduates high school because of his racists tattoos. He was killed by an African-American. As Danny said, "Well my conclusion is: Hate is baggage. Life's too short to be pissed off all the time. It's just not worth it." I mention this movie because watching this movie will be Sam's last incident before he is discharged.

But that's later. Sam and I finished up our initial conversation by me telling Sam he couldn't use any language that disparages others. I also told him that he had to follow all lawful orders. A lawful order adheres to Department of the Navy (DoN) and Department of Defense (DoD) regulations and policies. I told Sam that if he felt an order was unlawful he should complete the task first and then come to me. Before he left my office, I stressed he needed to knock before he comes in my office. Sam and I forged some minimal connection, on some level but definitely not friends. Sam left, and I continued with my work. I knew Sam would be back.

A few days later Sam has been back in my office numerous times. He knocked. I was never sure what was going to fall out of his mouth! One situation he said that someone, an African-American supervisor, gave him an order that didn't make sense. I had to measure what Sam believed doesn't make sense. I asked him what happened. He was late for morning muster. Sam had been late for all his assigned duties. He was verbally warned that the next time he was late he would receive some type of discipline. Discipline is not a legal process; it's for supervisors to keep good order and discipline. At sea, good order and discipline is essential for the carrier to accomplish its mission. We would have anarchy if there was not good order and discipline. I checked with his supervisor and got her side of the story. As I've said before there are three sides to every story. After talking to the supervisor, I found they both had some valid points. The supervisor was correct in her assessment of the issue, but she was wrong with how she wanted to correct Sam's behavior. Her remedy was to have him paint a door. Doesn't do much to correct Sam being late. Here's the way it should be handled. If a person is late for work, then the discipline must be related to the deficiency. If you have someone that comes in late then ensure they are counseled about work hours. Expectations must be set, and possible repercussions identified when the person is counseled. In Sam's case, he could take muster, and report a half hour early for work for one week. Needless to say, the supervisor was African-American which made the situation six times as bad in Sam's eyes. I did a bit of laser training for both and then sent them back to work. I knew that would not be the last time Sam would come to my office for help. Since he will not take orders from niggers, his words, why does he keep coming back to me? I tell him what he can and can't do based on his situation. As I stated earlier, Sam and I had some kind of connection and regardless of his derogatory language he and I had some enlightening chats. There are gaps between us because we are diverse. My job was to try to decrease gaps, not keep them the same or make them bigger. After the first time he came to my office, I gave him lawful orders. Sam did obey some of the orders I gave him. Maybe I'm in the category of 'I'm different from all the other niggers.' The exception to the rule according to Sam.

Sam was in my office three to four times a day at least. That was a bit excessive. I welcomed him each time, listened and told him what was true and not true. But his time in the Navy was about to end. On the carrier, we had Closed Circuit TV (CCTV). That was one of the ways we did training. That's how we watched satellite TV, movies from our CCTV studio, and watching our aircraft take off and land. Sailors could also have their own movies and watch them on a TV in their berthing, usually a small TV. One of the movies someone had was American History X. I've already described this movie in Chapter 4 with Steffan. It's amazing how this film is weaved throughout so many of my stories. Movie night was Sam's last night on the carrier as a free man. Males' berthing areas had up to between 70-100 Sailors divided into various size compartments. There are TVs about 20" in different places throughout the compartments. There was also VHS and a few DVD players. Don't forget all this occurred back between 2001-2005. Imagine 15-20 guys surrounding a 20" TV. I was told no one knew who the video belonged to nor did they know who put the video in to play. Of course, someone knows those things. The video starts out rather crazy and gets worse and then it gets better at the end, if you can wait that long. The group of guys initially watching was a diverse crowd. Some eyebrows were raised when the first nigger in the movie was spoken. Sam was thoroughly enjoying this movie because he had seen it numerous times. Some of the African-American Sailors left, and other Caucasians filled their spots. Some Caucasians also left because of the language. As the movie progresses more derogatory language and some serious violence. The violence is bad and of course, the violence is primarily toward African-Americans. More African-Americans left the TV viewing area, and now there was only a few African-Americans, more Caucasians and maybe a few Latinos. The following quote is only one of many that I could select. However, this one offends just about every race. Derek's mom was sickly and did not have male companionship. One man who was there for Sunday dinner (lunch) who was interested in dating his mom. Derek's problem with him; he was Jewish. Derek (Edward Norton) said:

"Oh it doesn't? You don't think I see what you're trying to do here? You think I'm gonna sit here and smile while some fuckin' kike tries to fuck my mother? It's never gonna happen Murray, fuckin' forget it, not on my watch, not while I'm in this family. I will fuckin' cut your Shylock nose off and stick it up your ass before I let that happen. Coming in here and poisoning my family's dinner with your Jewish, nigger-loving, hippie bullshit. Fuck you! Fuck you! Yeah, walk out, asshole, fuckin' Kabbalah reading motherfucker. Get the fuck out of my house."

During this tirade by Derek, one of the people watching this video knew almost every word and said it with Derek. He knew many quotes and said them right along with the movie. Sam. Unbelievable! I spent so much time and energy with him I just couldn't imagine him being that audacious. I think Sam thought if he was just repeating the derogatory words from this movie that he would not get in trouble. Or he knew, I told him, that if his behavior did not change now he would be discharged. He was so young; his parents had to sign for him to get in the Navy. He was also very immature and naïve. Those, however, are not things that gets someone discharged. Sam was not the only immature Sailor watching the movie. As Sam is spouting off the phrases, others are getting upset. And then it happened. No one claims to know who threw the first punch, but it didn't matter. Such a huge fight in a small compartment got out of hand quickly. From witness and perpetrator interviews they said people were thrown against racks, on the deck, which is steel, and the words exchanged just added fuel to the fire. There were fists thrown, people shoved into metal lockers, people pushed down on the floor and being kicked—it was totally out of control. It didn't last too long before our onboard security force got there, pulled people apart, and put a few in the brig to bring order and discipline. The brig is four or five actual jail cells to keep Sailors who had disobeyed orders or policies in an extreme way. As security was taking statements from those involved in the fight and witnesses it became clear why this happened. The movie, primarily Sam, and the others who talked along with the movie. After all the statements had been taken security provided me all the information so I could handle Sam who was the loudest most consistent Sailor talking along with the movie. I carefully read all the statements, and pretty much they all agreed that Sam was the instigator through his actions of repeating derogatory words even after he was told to stop. Sam was put in our brig, jail, for everyone's best interest. I had been to the brig numerous times before to do interviews. It was always weird to be locked in a cage with the alleged perpetrators, but they were in their own individual cells. The brig sometimes made Sailors a bit more cooperative which is why my interviews were usually more fruitful than if the Sailor comes to my office. I spoke to all involved and the witnesses to get a good picture of what happened. With all that, I finally speak with Sam. He told me what he did and didn't care who was listening to him parrot the movie. That's when I started being a bit sterner so I asked him why he thought what he did was not wrong. He was just repeating, and he didn't call anyone a derogatory name was his answer. Sam honestly believed he was right, and he wanted to know why he was in trouble. He figured since they were watching a movie with that language it must not be wrong. I told him that derogatory words are just that, and he didn't need to say the words to anyone.

Sam was only in the brig for less than a day prior to his legal process I was in my office when my door flung open, like I first met Sam, and in came Sam out of uniform and blurted out he wanted to talk to me before his legal process began. He ran from his security detail who were only one step behind him. I tell security to wait just a second, so I can tell

Sam why he needed to leave my office and come back in the proper uniform and he best knock. I told security what the plan was, and they did as I requested. About five minutes later I heard a knock, and it was Sam. We didn't have that much time, so I asked him why he wanted to see me. He began by apologizing to me because of all the time I spent with him, but it didn't work. Sam said it is too hard to change. Imagine my surprise and I just hope I didn't physically let my jaw drop. And the big shocker was his next admission. "Thank ya for listening to me," I told him it was my job and my pleasure working with him. I told him that during his legal proceedings I would have to tell the truth, and I wouldn't be on his side. Sam didn't say anything else. All this took about two minutes. I delivered him back to security. His legal proceedings only took about one minute. He ended up with three days in the brig on bread and water. Because of his actions, Sam was to be sent off the ship immediately, after he was released from the brig. What a few weeks with Sam. I did enjoy the time I spent with Sam because it helped me grow as an EOA/DO and more importantly as a person. That may sound counterintuitive so let me explain what I mean. Talking with those different from me makes my life bigger and better. It doesn't matter if I'm talking to someone who hates me because I think when they get to know me I'm just a good 'ole country girl.

Being from a small town in Kentucky I was not phased, personally, by what Sam believed and said. I used to get called that, plus monkey, spook and much more. I must clarify that I was never disrespected in my hometown. When we traveled for softball or basketball games some Caucasians were open and honest about how they felt about me being an African-American. My friends always had my back.

Those who are socialized to hate and go out into the world have no idea how to interact with others. They need someone to try and change their perspectives using patience and honesty. I did that with all the young racists and discovered some positive things about me as a person and discovered some perspectives I needed to change. Shouldn't we all treat others with respect remembering they are people too? Isn't that how we should live life?

CHAPTER 7

Wrong Conversations?

THAT'S NOT WHAT I MEANT!

Successful communications don't require any skill or ability. It happens when the communicator is confident and determined to be clear, concise, and succinct. The business environment is a great example which really requires successful communication. Additionally, keeping respect up front always gives an excellent result.

The communication process is underutilized. It requires some work; this process can be for everyday like our social conversations. The process starts when we encode and decode messages based on their tone, their medium, white noise, and most importantly our filters. What are our filters? Filters come from our socialization process from Chapter 1. Our beliefs, values, knowledge, and more are how we send and receive messages. What

do you see happening in this conversation below? The picture explains the dynamics of the conversation without words, because of non-verbs.

The picture demonstrates the power of non-verbs. Non-verbs (non-verbal) make up most of our face to face communication. What's going on here in this communication? First, they are in each

other's personal space so they must be very familiar with each other. The receiver's facial expression and gestures say, 'I'm not buying what you are selling' and, 'Are you serious?' Gestures from both men lead me to believe they are serious about the subject of the message. The guy's face you can see is probably the supervisor to this other guy. I say that because face guy has his hand on his hip and that's a classic sign of being in charge. My observations give me enough information to see how both men felt about the conversation frustrated and heated. There are a couple more non-verbs so give it a try. Here's why awareness of non-verbs are significant. We communicate 93% of our message through non-verbs. 7% of communication is the words we use. It is worth breaking down the 93% so we can fully grasp how we communicate. 38%

non-verbs are expressed through tone of voice and 55% through facial expressions, proxemics, posture, etc. When I discovered the power of non-verbs, they changed the way I communicated.

Different cultures communicate with their own style. The following non-verbs are generalizations, stereotypes, of observed behaviors exhibited by a culture. Of course, not everyone in a culture behaves the same, but these are excellent guides when you are not familiar with a culture. Culture not only includes demographics but also the region, part of the country, or even part of a state. People living in Southern CA are different than those in Northern CA. East coast is known for hurried lives that ignore others. In contrast, West Coast is laid back and wants to include everyone. Finally, I'm from KY, which many people think we are in the south however we are central east. We do share many of the behaviors of the South speaking in our slow drawl.

Non-verbs can derail an otherwise good conversation, especially when dealing with different cultures. The following information was collected from various reputable resources. I'll start with eye contact. Eye contact is one of the most important non-verbs to understand. In the U.S. eye contact indicates respect, honesty, interest, and defines power, status, and class. Western cultures believe that eye contact means respect and truth. African-Americans tend to use more eye contact when speaking. The Middle East cultures also believe that eye contact indicates truthfulness. They tend to make prolonged eye contact which makes some other people nervous. Some in the U.S.A. consider a gaze as aggression, or, defiance, or confrontation. Native Americans, Japanese, Latin Americans, and Caribbean's all avoid eye contact as a way to show respect. One note, in Latin America there are some country specifics for non-verbs. Our eyes convey our emotions even though we may be saying something entirely different than our words. That's important to remember when making eye contact.

The importance of understanding eye contact and business success. Jason, a U.S. businessman, is in Latin America to see if his organization can do business there. As Jason is speaking with Mary from Brazil, he notices Mary is not making eye contact with him. Jason is not well versed in cultural differences and gets upset with Mary because Jason believes she is not interested in what is being said. He traveled a long way to have this meeting, so Jason expected Mary to give his proposal serious attention. Jason gets angry and raises his voice asking Mary why she's not paying attention. Mary replied by paraphrasing what Jason had said so far. As Mary is leaving the meeting, she tells Jason that she is no longer interested in doing business with Jason's organization because he apparently knows nothing about the Brazilian culture.

Touch can send the wrong message in many different cultures. In the Middle East they usually don't use left hands because that's the hand used for toilet functions. Additionally, in the Middle East, they don't approve of touching between men and women unless married. However, hugs and holding hands between men is acceptable. I tend to touch people when I talk to them; but I really don't know if that's from being from a small town in Kentucky.

Another non-verb is paralanguage, meaning any vocal features when speaking. There are three dimensions. The first dimension is vocal characterizers. A yell, yawn, or laughter. Next, vocal qualifiers include tone and rhythm. Volume is another qualifier. A loud voice in Middle Eastern cultures mean strength and in Germany, it means confidence and authority. Vocal segregates are the third qualifier. Uh-huh, ooh, and uh indicate doubt or approval.

Proxemics, physical distance, is widely different between cultures. Americans' proxemics are relatively rigid; social space is between four to twelve feet. In Latin America and the Middle East, they are much closer to four feet when they speak. When Jason goes to the Middle East and begins a conversation, Mustafa may be approximately two to three feet away as the conversation starts. Jason can't step back from Mustafa because he got into Jason's personal space. Jason is totally uncomfortable and not paying attention to the conversation. He should have known that people in the Middle East stand close when they speak. To get business done, Jason must deal with it.

When I was talking to the racists, especially when talking to Steffan and Sam, my tone started out a bit harsh but, settled into a friendlier tone. I needed to establish myself as the one directing the conversation because I never knew what was going to fall out of their mouths. Additionally, I leaned in and made eye contact, which neither were expecting. I was also about one foot away from them. In their cases, I had to keep them off guard, so they would not have time to think about what to say. I used my knowledge of non-verbs to make my communications for effective.

To be a highly effective communicator knowing a culture's tendencies is only part of the communication equation. The other part is understanding the purpose of the conversation, so you can participate at a level that leads both of you to the purpose of the conversation. It doesn't have to be serious, it could be as simple as talking about football (soccer). When talking football with someone it's good to know something about his or her culture.

I have no problem or concern speaking to those who don't look like me. Conversations about race are one of the most challenging and controversial discussions, yet rewarding. One reason they are so tough is they become very personal. That adds several layers to an already supercharged situation. Results in strained and incoherent conversations with no real focus leads to miscommunications. One of my Admirals, CEO, told me I had a gift in how I could relate to anyone about anything even if it were incongruent to my beliefs. I seem to put myself where they were and speak to them from their point of view. My beliefs have nothing to do with educating the ignorant. He said I readily identified with the person I was speaking with, which made the person thoroughly relaxed. I am sincerely interested in every conversation and my goal is to ensure the other person knows I'm interested. As an Equal Opportunity Advisor, I knew I needed to understand their circumstances. Understanding comes from openness.

It is not easy to take an unpopular position especially when race is involved. For instance, I spoke with some Caucasians who were concerned about being treated unfairly. I checked it out and found Caucasians were treated unfairly, but some African-Americans were upset. It is hard for some in a job like mine to take the high road so to speak and take the difficult yet correct stance. Explaining decisions without emotions is what works for me. I can't allow the emotions of those in distress to get me off my goal of the conversation. Sometimes a person feeds off the emotions of others and that derails a conversation. A couple of times I have gotten swept up in emotions and I made some serious mistakes in a conversation. It's hard to recover. As I was once told 'you can't splice life.' It took me a minute to figure that out. I am not saying that I was or am perfect, but I did the right thing no matter what. I endured many fellow Chief Petty Officers (CPOs) despising me because of a wrong committed by our fellow CPOs. Some people in my position did not pursue their fellow Chief Petty Officers, (CPO), but wrong is wrong even if everyone agrees and right is right even if no one agrees. One of the most challenging situations for me was ensuring my fellow CPOs were held to the highest standard expected of CPOs. That is an ultimate test of integrity. I had to be very forthright with my explanations.

A person who seeks out enriching conversations is a trend setter and would be an excellent leader and a model employee or friend. There are not enough of these dialogues because some people don't know what to say or how to say it without being disrespectful. Everyone must be prepared for some disparaging remarks about his or her culture. It's how you respond that makes an impression on someone. However, if the truth is not told, then it will always be uncomfortable between people. We talk around issues and don't get to the real stuff. For example, hate exists, and minorities know that there are epithets they don't and shouldn't accept. But the epithets are said and again I say don't get caught up in emotions. When epithets start flying it gets crazy, but the recipient should consider the source and know it could be ignorance that's drives those words. It is sometimes difficult to begin an enlightened conversation, after epithets, but I have a list of over 60 questions and statements that will spark a discussion. Having a discussion with someone who just called you an epithet is probably not first on your mind, but it is a great way to catch someone off guard. A question I often ask is "What does that mean?" Other questions are great when beginning a conversation with someone who doesn't look like you. Here is a sample of questions and statements that will start a chat and who knows where it may go from there.

Name three of your favorite things. Name a time you felt fear.

What's your proudest moment?

What's the most difficult thing you've done?

Remember you may be trying to start a conversation with someone who just called you an epithet or said something ignorant about you or your culture or you just want to start a conversation. Those statements and questions above will hopefully take the sting out of what was said. Conversations should be fruitful, fun and illuminating. When I had to talk to the racists, my frame of mind was to learn and help them grow and find a way I could grow. Not everyone will grow from an amazing conversation, but the point is that you tried to make a difference.

Mastering communication requires active listening. There is a difference between hearing and listening. Hearing is an involuntary process that is merely sound sent to the brain. Listening indicates a person is taking what they hear and start understanding what is being said. But there's a higher level of listening which is Active Listening.

Active Listening takes work but, ensures a total grasp on the sender's message. Head nodding, some eye contact, paraphrasing, parroting or repeating all show the sender that the receiver is understanding and interested in the conversation. Without Active Listening, communications would go wrong almost every time.

Active Listening is not that easy, it requires the receiver of a message to work hard listening. When showing the sender everything is being received, care must be taken that the receiver is not doing too much. Excessive head nodding or paraphrasing can give the   sender the impression that the receiver is just going through the motions and not listening. Here's a true story about just going through the motions of active listening.

I was the receiver when a Sailor, Tricia, needed my help. Tricia was telling me her story and I was head nodding, repeating, paraphrasing, and leaning in toward her. Being a good active listener so I thought. Twenty minutes later I realized that I didn't know what she was talking about. I was so into active listening that I wasn't listening. I stopped her and started paraphrasing a bit and asked questions and I got back on track. Asking questions is another great active listening tool. It's easy to get into a rhythm with head nodding and repeating. Be aware.

Getting out of the zone of head nodding there are some questions that will make sense to both in the conversation and saves the listener. What did you say? Not the best way to try and get back into a conversation. These are types of good questions:

When did you say that was?

How would you characterize that? Why do you feel this way?

Wrong conversations can happen because the people involved are ignorant about the other person, not active listening, or using the wrong non-verb. It's not possible to know everyone's background but you can quickly and easily find out something about a person. My Ask and Reveal questions are perfect for that. Be eager and excited about getting to know someone and maybe learning something about yourself during the same conversation. Surprise yourself!

CHAPTER 8

Seriously, is that the only seat?

ATE 20A. Think about the gate area in the airport. Think about where you don't drive or the neighborhoods you don't go. One more, what do you think about when you hear African-American suspect in crime against an African-American? These create uncomfortable situations but why?

It's all about our stereotypes; again, this word invades our lifestyle. Allow me to explain using the gate area in the airport. When I travel, I like to get to the gate area early. On this occasion when I get to the area, there are a lot of people there already, and seats are limited. I prefer the end seats because I can put my bag on the floor and not take away another seat. However, this time, I'm out of luck. Now I must decide who I might have to sit by, and there are only a few options. As I scan the seats some people are looking at me as I'm looking at them to find an empty seat. There's one between two young Caucasian men, one by an African-American, and one by an older Caucasian guy. Decisions, decisions. I decide to sit by the older Caucasian guy mainly because the seat was the closest I could get to the line. No big deal I thought, except when I sat down, the older Caucasian man moved to the seat between the two young Caucasians. He may have just moved to get more comfortable, but I'm not sure. See this has happened to me before and I can tell when someone is uncomfortable with me sitting by or standing near them. That used to bother me, but I learned it is not me they are shying away from but who they think I am. Their stereotype of me. I came to realize when that happens I have one of two choices. Choice one is to get upset and treat a Caucasian who sat beside me the same way I've been treated. Choice two, accept that it will continue to happen and don't take it personally. I've gone with choice two since then, and now I'll take any seat by anyone.

Here's an easier example to imagine or you may have seen. When I traveled in my Navy uniform, I would sit by other people in uniform if it was possible. Why? Because they looked like me, not exactly of course but military is military. No matter what service we all had things in common. Sameness makes us feel safe, and we can be who we are.

Working, shopping or even eating dinner at a restaurant, English only speakers are uneasy when people are speaking a different language. There are automatic responses when people are around those speaking a different language. In the Navy I dealt with this too much. The workplace is where I heard the most about people being upset with others for speaking another language during lunch or when talking to each other at their pukas. What statement did I hear most often? They may be talking about me. Automatic response one. I told them neither they nor their personal lives were that exciting that people only needed to talk about them. I additionally told them they thought too highly of themselves. That may have been a bit harsh, but it made the point. Another statement I hear is 'why don't they learn to speak English.' I'm not sure obdurate people don't really care what language a person speaks it's all about their race and/or ethnicity. It is about sameness. It's the same for being anywhere around those that English is their second or third language. For businesses, the EEOC is the organization that provides guidance about English in the workplace. It states that unless for a business necessity, employees can speak other than English. Smart business is to use someone's first language when marketing and hiring in that demographic. That is especially important with the global market and society. English is the language spoken throughout the world especially in business. However, there are many other beautiful languages, and after all our great country was founded by immigrants that spoke different languages.

I believe the Caucasian guy at Gate 20A was uncomfortable and that's why he changed seats. I also made some Navy leaders uncomfortable, both as an African-American female and as an Equal Opportunity/Diversity Officer. That worked to my advantage and my detriment. The disadvantage prohibited me from doing a few things that our organization needed to improve our business culture and environment. I use the words culture and environment separately because they are different things. Culture refers to the identity of the organization. The environment is the feel of an organization. I could tell when there was a terrible work environment because it could be seen and heard. An environment can be created by a like-minded group of people not an entire organization. The Girl Scouts have their own environment; a police department does also, both environments have their own feel. I had an advantage in my environment because I could talk to people others felt uncomfortable around and usually they're the ones who know what's going on. Therefore, I was able to get more accurate in-depth information from an environment and what was working or not.

Here's a prime example. There was a situation that made my immediate supervisor, Ronald, uneasy. Ronald had made up his mind about the issue before any inquiry could take place. An African- American officer received his yearly fitness report and was not pleased about the content. Johnie, the officer, believed his fitness report was obviously different when compared to Caucasian officers' fitness reports. It was not so much the rating that upset Johnie, but it was the content. So, he came to me with his concerns and wanted to file a formal complaint against our VADM, Tom because he was the bottom signature; Johnie's reporting senior. A reporting senior had the final decision on what would and would not be in a fitness report. A complaint against senior staff is a huge deal in the Navy and was reportable to our reporting senior's leader, like a Chairman of the Board. Johnie told me what his concerns were and how he wanted to proceed. I had to tell my bosses right away what was going on, but I found that they already knew. Johnie's supervisors told Tom and just as I was finishing up with Johnie I got a call from Ronald asking me to come to his office. I was totally prepared, like always dealing with senior leaders, and I was anxious to begin the conversation.

There was a Navy study done that proved African-American males evaluations contained words like, "aggressive vice assertive", or "dominant leader vice strong leader." A chapter in the book Managing Diversity in the Military was devoted to Navy fitness report disparities between White and Black Officers. Those same results are why Johnie filed his complaint. Ronald, and I went over Johnie's fitness report, and I pointed out what Johnie felt was wrong. Ronald stated he didn't see anything wrong with the fitness report. During my inquiry, I heard different things from Johnie's supervisors than from his subordinates. I reviewed other items to verify his fitness report comments, and I could only affirm a couple of the descriptions of Johnie's performance. The other comments appeared to be biased.

Ronald still couldn't understand why Johnie would be filing a complaint. Before responding to Ronald's comment, I took a deep breath and said, sir, you wouldn't know because you can pass for Caucasian. The only thing that gives you away not being 100% Caucasian is the shape of your eyes which appear to be Japanese. Johnie cannot pass for anything other than who he is and that's how it should be, but it's not. Ronald looked at me like I had two heads, but he couldn't say anything because I was right. Johnie looked very different than his superiors and Ronald looked like his peers. Most African-Americans can't blend in with Caucasians. It's the 'you don't look like me' issue which brings in unconscious bias and stereotype. I walked out of Ronald's office and went back to mine. After about two minutes I was called to Tom's, the boss, office about this situation. Of course, I thought I was in trouble for what I said to Ronald. To my surprise, Tom agreed that Johnie's fitness report should be changed. They changed his fitness report, and that uncomfortable situation was over. This situation is a fantastic time to use this quote from the movie To Kill a Mocking Bird. Here's the scene Gregory Peck – Atticus and his daughter Scout were talking about her first day of school. She was fighting in her dress and as she's scrapping she beats up a boy. What Atticus says next is beyond profound. Look and listen. Atticus said that you can't understand a person until you walk around in their skin and see things from their way. How do you walk around in someone else's skin, not merely their shoes? One, get to know the person beyond superficial things. The only way that is going to happen is taking time to talk to the individual. Ronald didn't know anything about Johnie making it hard for Ronald to understand Johnie's concerns. When we try to imprint ourselves on others it will not work because we are all different, thank goodness. We must stop putting our values, beliefs, behaviors onto others.

Switching gears, going back to the carrier. Those practicing religion created issues for some. Different worship liturgies and beliefs made people uncomfortable. Some people believed others should not be able to practice their religious rites. Christians worship on Sunday morning, which aligned with the ship's Sunday morning schedule. Jews worship Friday sundown to Saturday sundown. Their religious customs sometimes were curtailed. Muslims, who are Islamic, pray five times a day and they worshipped on Fridays at noon. That was in direct conflict with our work schedule. Sailors could ask others to cover for them during any worship service. Usually no one had a problem covering for Christians who happened to be working Sunday morning. Remember we work seven days a week on the carrier when we are out to sea. Jews did sometimes have a hard time worshipping because it was prime time work schedule.

Muslims, rarely if ever could worship because their Thuhr prayer time, is just after noon, which corresponds to their worship time on Friday. However, we did give every faith the opportunity to practice as long as the mission was not impacted.

Others who were Agnostic, Atheist or other faiths sometimes had to work while others worshipped. Unfortunately, they were also forced to hear a Christian prayer over the 1MC every night and a prayer before each event. They could not escape it which made some uncomfortable. All I could do for them is to help them deal with the praying by giving them ideas of what to do during the prayer. We did our best to make sure no one abused their worship time.

There was one young Sailor that said he experienced religious discrimination, but he was not correct. Pete refused to work on Friday because that was his worship day. Pete had been onboard for over a year and this is the first time he acted out regarding his faith. He took his concerns straight to our CO (Captain) which was his right to do. The Captain couldn't talk to Pete until he talked to me about his issues. Pete came to my office and told me his story about his religion. It is called the Nation of Yahweh which is considered a hate group by Southern Poverty Law Center (SPLC), an organization that tracks hate groups, because of its doctrine. Yahweh ben Yahweh founded the Nation of Yahweh-believing that Jesus and the 12 disciplines were African-American. They are against Caucasians and say all Caucasians should be murdered. Their Sabbath day is on the seventh day, sundown Friday to sundown Saturday. Pete wanted the whole day on Fridays, which would only be the sixth day of their week. Certain religions believe Sunday is the first day of the week. After I had conducted my research, Pete and I went back to the Captain's office. I told the Captain what I learned and based on the research we didn't recognize Nation of Yahweh as a religion we could have on the ship. Pete admitted he followed the doctrine of the Nation of Yahweh meaning he had to be discharged because he was an active member of a hate group. That was hard to explain to those who knew Pete because he had made his case to his friends who became sea lawyers, previously mentioned. We suspected Pete wanted to get out of the Navy and he found the best way to get out.

Religion will always be an emotional and controversial discussion.

One more religion we had to deal with was Wicca. Wicca makes quite a few people uncomfortable because they believed it was witchcraft. There is a lot of wrong information about Wicca, so I'll tell what I learned directly from a Wiccan. First, Wicca is not satanic nor is it witchcraft although there are witches just not in the traditional or movie sense. *A Witch seeks to control the forces within him or herself that make life possible in order to live wisely and well, without harm to others, and in harmony with Nature. (part of Principle VIII)* - Wicca Janey explained what they believed. Wicca is a very diverse religion, so it has various forms of worship. There are 13 principles of Wicca, but I'll only cover a couple. Most people don't know that Wiccans believe in God and that Jesus is their Saviour. Wiccans use scripture to guide them. Janey shared a couple of principles:

Principle I -*We practice rites to attune ourselves with the natural rhythm of life forces marked by the phases of the Moon and the*

seasonal quarters and cross-quarters. They reference Deuteronomy 4:19.

Principle XII - **We do not accept the concept of "absolute evil," nor do we worship any entity known as "Satan" or "the Devil" as defined by Christian Tradition. We do not seek power through the suffering of others, nor do we accept the concept that personal benefits can only be derived by denial to another.** They reference 2nd Corinthians 11:13-15

Approving Wicca as a religion on the ship was necessary because they deserved to practice their beliefs. I thought the truth about Wicca would quell the misconceptions.

I could go on with uncomfortable issues like these. Being uncomfortable indicates the situation should be a learning moment and possibly change a perspective. Be open-minded. Be willing to assess why you are uncomfortable and share that with others. I've felt uneasy in quite a few situations. Sometimes it took me a while to acknowledge my stereotypes and to put them in check. I talked to friends about my uneasiness and asked them to be truthful with me. Was I blind to the facts or was I stubborn? Eventually, I had to decide for myself that I was being trivial allowing my stereotypes to negatively affect me. Sometimes it's just that simple.

CHAPTER 9

Extremists May Be In Your Town Right Now

HATE IS A POWERFUL ATTENTION getting word that may turn some off. In Chapter 16 I identify a few of the religious hate groups and you'll read how they take religion and turn it into hate. For this book I will use hate or extremists group interchangeably. It's important to note that there are extremist's groups that have nothing to do with hate. According to the SPLC there are 917 active hate groups in the United States as of the end of 2016. They are passively active in some situations, and others are very vocal. Do you have a hate group in your town?

Extremists groups must recruit. Their recruitment of females doesn't seem to be a priority. Members of hate groups look for those kids who are loners, don't feel connected to family, are seeking to be part of something; they are starving for positive attention and so much more. When a young man or young lady joins a hate group, they are courted so he or she stay. The group will invite them to a picnic, concert, to go camping, even do some love matchmaking. Hate group members are very loyal to each other and will never allow one of their own to be victimized. That practice assures the recruit that he or she is in the right place.

Hate groups cause terror. There are legal distinctions between extremists and terrorist's groups. They both recruit the same using because they are targeting the same group of people.

Extremists groups have recording studios and make a massive number of CDs. That's something a young kid or teen would get into for sure. Here are two websites that you can hear the music and see how much swag they have available. On Label 56 and 88 Records, you can sample some of their songs for free. It's worth a listen. Of course, I listened to a couple on Label 56, there are so many, and I could only catch a few words and they were not pleasant. Not only do the CDs make money some extremists groups have concerts that are wild.

From music to print. There are publishers that are looking for controversial content. The Turner Diaries, said to be the plan Timothy McVeigh used for the Oklahoma City Bombing, is a great example of how extremists' groups can get their message out. Barricadebooks.com is the publisher of the Turner Diaries and states on their website, *"Noone needs the first amendment to write about how cute newborn babies are or to publish a recipe for strawberry shortcake. The first amendment was not intended for innocuous ideas or popular points of view. We at Barricade Books are committed to protecting the rights of serious authors to express even the most unpopular, outrageous and offensive ideas. Only then is total freedom of expression guaranteed."* There are other publishers, but most are only known to the hate groups.

I visited many hate group websites, and initially some of them look harmless. Once I started going further into the website it was evident what that group stood for and who they hated. Those sites are inviting with music and colorful, busy scenes. Some of these sites are so good I had a hard time identifying them as an extremist group. That's the beauty of those websites because a possible recruit could get caught up in the group before he or she realizes that's going on with their new friends.

These groups are also very good at misquoting the Bible for their use. They love the Old Testament because it suits their purposes.

For example, slave ownership is permitted, however, slaves had the opportunity to be released from their owner. The groups leave out the parts that don't suit their purpose. Using the Bible makes a group more likable and legitimate in friends and families' eyes leading to their initial approval of their kids' friend choice.

The Caucasian hate group, Racist Skinheads, is the group that will be my focus. "Racist Skinheads form a particularly violent element of the Caucasian supremacist movement, and have often been referred to as the "shock troops" of the hoped-for revolution. The classic Skinhead look is a shaved head, Doc Martens boots, jeans with suspenders and an array of typically racist tattoos." https://www.splcenter.org/fighting-hate/ extremist-files/ideology/racist-skinhead This group is notorious for their vocal hatred of everyone. Shock troops are specially trained, specifically chosen, and equipped to carry out an assault. The Doc Marten boots racist skinheads wear are ladder laced, distinguishing them from regular Dr. Martens like I wear. Here's a picture of racist skinhead ladder laces. The Doc Martens are an essential part of a racist skinhead ensemble. In addition to their Docs, racist skinheads also have steel toed boots, so they can have boot parties. These parties consist of a beat down to the ground, and then the racist skinheads start kicking the person on the ground with their steel toed boots. Steffan, from the carrier, said he was part of a racist skinhead group back in Minnesota. The original skinheads were formed in the 1960s in the United Kingdom. They are a group that listens to their own style of music and have shaved heads. Just like other symbols, racists take something good and make it their own ergo the term racists skinheads.

The next group I'd like to highlight are African-American Separatists. *African-American separatists typically oppose integration and racial intermarriage, and they want separate institutions -- or even a separate nation -- for African-Americans. Most forms of African-American separatism are strongly anti-Caucasian and anti-Semitic, and a number of religious versions assert that African-Americans are the Biblical "chosen people" of God.* https://www.splcenter.org/fighting-hate/extremist-files/ideology/black-separatist These groups are sometimes linked to the Nation of Islam. The Nation of Islam is an anti-everything. Louis Farrakhan, as the leader of the Nation of Islam, said the group was strongly anti-Caucasian, anti-Semitic, anti-Catholic, and anti-homosexual. The Nation of Islam is not traditional Islam. I have not encountered anyone in the Nation of Islam, but I had personal experience with African-Americans who hated Caucasians. There were a few instances of graffiti targeted at whites back on the aircraft carrier. The New Black Panther Party also hates Jews and Caucasians. They also stand for violence against police. Additionally, I heard African-Americans talk negatively about Caucasians, and that did cause some fights when we were in port back on the ship. Black Lives Matter (BLM) is not related to any of the above hate groups. BLM is a movement to protest Black Americans mistreatment in the justice system.

Additionally, on the ship I was disliked by some African-Americans. I conducted a few investigations involving blacks and whites, I concluded, that some whites were innocent of the charges. I received menacing notes under my door or had African-Americans stop speaking to me or even having someone post derogatory notes about me in work areas. I took all that as a compliment because they noticed I was doing my job regardless of any backlash. That meant I would do the same for them if they needed my help.

The oldest hate group in the U.S. is the Ku Klux Klan (KKK). According to Public Broadcast Status (PBS) website, "the KKK was formed in Pulaski, TN on December 24th, 1865. It was originally formed as a social club for former Confederate soldiers but later evolved into a terrorist organization." http://www.pbs.org/wgbh/americanexperience/features/grant-kkk/ People don't typically think about hate groups such as the KKK as a terrorist group and I think it's the definition many forget about. Terrorism is, according to Merriam-Webster, the systematic use of terror as a means of coercion. Remember there are legal definitions for extremists and terrorist's groups. The Klan's priority was to kill as many African-Americans as possible in any way that was most violent. The KKK became a hooded hate group in 1868 and not only focused on African-Americans but whites, known as whiggers, who were married to or hanging around with blacks. They grew to hate, homosexuals, immigrants and recently Catholics. They believed a lot in the Old Testament because some of that fits their ideology. The KKK was known for their lynching's. Lynching's were heinous and caused a lot of terror because they happened at any time anywhere. What I find most interesting is that President Abraham Lincoln was a Republican and the Republican party, sort of, supported the end of slavery and creating a world that whites and blacks could live harmoniously. The republican party of late, around 1972, became less minority focused and more homeland type focused. The KKK is known for some of the worst acts against African-Americans. KKK members were in law enforcement, in the court systems, pervasive throughout communities, particularly in businesses. Additionally, many members of the KKK were Protestant, however not all Protestants were in the KKK.

Extremist groups love to recruit military personnel and law enforcement professionals. The Department of Defense's hate group policy is very restrictive and definitive. I talked about this earlier, but extremist groups want military personnel who possess certain skills, talents, and access. The most sought-after personnel are logistics, supply, weapons, with security clearances, leadership, explosives access, and much more. Discipline in a hate group is paramount; that's another reason why hate groups like military personnel. Extremists also demand loyalty to their beliefs. A disciplined group is usually a loyal group. Military personnel are disciplined. Law enforcement personnel have many of the same skills, talents, and abilities plus more.

There are some charismatic leaders of these groups or they just talk a good game about hate and become the voice of hate. *Robert Spencer is the director of the Jihad Watch blog and co-founder of Stop Islamization of America, Robert Spencer is one of America's most prolific and vociferous anti-Muslim propagandists.* https://www.splcenter.org/fighting-hate/extremist-files/individual/robert-spencer Mr. Spencer's stance is that Islam is a violent religion and jihadist just follow the religion. He believes that Islam was hijacked by jihadist and there are not enough good Muslims to stop the jihadist. Mr. Spencer has a blog called Jihadist Watch, and he uses it to spread his hate toward Muslims. He talks about Islam as though he is an expert, but Mr. Spencer has never formally studied Islam so what he knows about this religion is self-taught; he has no documentation for most of what he espouses. People like Robert Spencer are why hate will always be around. When ignorant people hear things like what Mr. Spencer espouses, people will believe it because they don't know, it is wrong. Ignorance is bliss?

Here's some truth about Islam. Islam is not only a religion but a way of life. Muslims practice Islam a religion of mercy, forgiveness, and peace. There are approximately 1 billion Muslims and the clear majority are not terrorists. Islam consists of Muslims of different races, ethnicities, and cultures.

I was fortunate enough to spend two weeks with an Arab-American Muslim family. I didn't know anything about Islam or Arab-Americans.

During my two weeks with them I went to a Mosque during one of their prayers. They gave me a Qur'an. The women explained why they worship behind the men. The men will not be distracted from Allah by looking at the women. The women also clarified that they are cherished by Muslim men in general and it is a cultural thing when women are oppressed.

A verse from my Qur'an:

Al-Hujurat 49:10 The Believers are but a single Brotherhood: so make peace and reconciliation between your two (contending) brothers; and fear Allah, that you may receive Mercy.

Another verse from the Qur'an:

Ta-Ha 20:130 Therefore be patient with what they say, and celebrate the praises of your Lord, before the rising of the sun, and before it's setting; yes, celebrate them for part of the hours of the night, and at the sides of the day: that you may have joy.

From peace to another extremist leader Malik Shabazz. Mr. Shabazz is black, and he is a racist. He has a well-documented history of violently attacking Jews with words. Mr. Shabazz also believes that Caucasians have an innate evil. He was the leader of the New Black Panther Party in 2001. Mr. Shabazz alleged that 9/11 terrorist attacks were a Jewish conspiracy. He then took that claim to start an extensive series of protests. He did some good by founding the Black Lawyers for Justice, and one of their missions is to ensure that blacks know how to deal with the police. This organization also organizes rallies all over the country. Those demonstrations are in areas that have recently experienced some controversial action with police and blacks or to make some serious statements. Mr. Shabazz holds nothing back when he gives his opinions.

There's no mistaking what he thinks, and his willingness to verbally attack those in power shows he will not respect anyone, regardless of color, whose actions are in support of Caucasians and Jews.

In times of strife and discontentment, extremists' language and ideology are used to galvanize those who hate. The former governor of Alabama George Wallace had the backing of the most recognizable hate group, the KKK, during the 1960's when racism was rampant. Governor Wallace was known for these three phrases, *"Segregation now, segregation tomorrow, segregation forever."* Those thoughts didn't go away for many people, and that's why there are 917 active hate groups across the U.S. To combat extremist speech and action, use language and examples of the opposite of what those who think and believe hate is right. A good question is to ask them why they hate and keeping asking until you get to five why's. That works.

Islamophobia. Muslims are attacked, verbally and physically, every day, literally every day. Those incidents have been documented in the news. Many in the U.S., primarily Caucasians, want all Muslims gone because of the actions of radical extremists and extremist groups. Following an Islamophobias' thinking all Muslims are evil. That's based on Muslims of varying races and ethnic groups. Islamophobia also exists because of ignorance about Islam and Muslims in general. According to Islamic Statistics website, there are 350 million Muslims, who are Christians in secret. I have a Qur'an, and I've read some of it to understand those different than me. The Qur'an parallels the Bible and Torah although there are some significant differences.

Here's some truth about Islam. Islam is not only a religion but a way of life. Muslims practice Islam a religion of mercy, forgiveness, and peace. There are approximately 1 billion Muslims and the vast majority are not terrorists. Islam consists of Muslims of different races, ethnicities, and cultures.

I spent two weeks with an Arab-American family who were Muslims. I learned the difference between culture and religion and in some areas, it is stark. I went to a Mosque during one of their prayers. The women explained why they worship behind the men. The men are not distracted from Allah by looking at the women.

This Islamophobia is nothing more than hate; hate based on generalizations and ignorance creating stereotypes. The jihadist believes in hate, and they are of all ethnic groups. Matter of fact, some of the jihadists don't even know what's in the Qur'an.

We all remember 9/11. That was committed by extremists with pure hate in their hearts. They evoked Allah's name and the Qur'an as their reason to kill others. That is how the KKK justified killing African-Americans by using various verses from the Bible. ISIS (Islamic State of Iraq and Syria) is entirely different init's goals and purposes. It began in October 2006. ISIS is a splinter group from al-Qaeda. Their goal is to create an Islamic state, the caliph, governed by Sharia or Islamic Law. What makes ISIS so dangerous is how good they are at recruiting individuals online to carry out their ideology. They don't care who you are; ISIS will indoctrinate, radicalize you to their beliefs and thinking. They may ask you to carry out some form of terrorism. The Islamic Supreme Council of America has excellent information about ISIS. Like other extremist's groups, ISIS recruits the lonely, abused, misused, wanting fame and needing to belong to something. ISIS has a cause, and that brings people to them because people need a cause. ISIS is using all the tools available to them to draw people to their ranks. Social media has helped ISIS spread their terrorist acts throughout the world. They are very adept at recruiting those who are not students of Islam, even though he or she doesn't know what it means to be Islamic, and that says something.

Two issues Muslims face here in the U.S. are prayers and Muslim women dressing in their hijab, niqab, and burkas. The females dress is both cultural or religious, and it is important to them. Just like many people in Texas wear cowboy hats and boots or devout Jewish males who wear their yarmulke those are comparable to the reason why Muslim women should be able to wear their traditional clothing. Muslims must perform Salat (pray) five times a day but that is not always feasible. If necessity causes a Muslim to miss a prayer, then he or she should pray that prayer sooner rather than later. I've heard people complain about Muslims saying their prayers, which are the second pillar of Islam. The complaint is their time away from work, although it is minimal. On the aircraft carrier I accidently walked upon a Muslim man saying his prayers in a corner of the workplace. It was quiet and out of the way a perfect space for him to unite his mind, body, and soul to make a connection with Allah. There is a massive disparity between what people know and their ignorance of Muslims' cultures, religion, and their desires to live peacefully. In my over 28 years of dealing with people, I know for sure that people are not comfortable with those who don't look like them, don't dress like them, don't talk like them and who are just different. This is what I dealt with on the ship. Christians had Sunday mornings for worship. The Jewish sabbath begins after the end of the work day on Friday at sunset. Some people believe Friday prayers and worship for Muslims in the middle of the work day is not quite fair.

We fear what we don't know or fully understand. Most hate groups rarely do any research about why they hate the groups they choose. They regurgitate what they were told by parents, grandparents, friends, the news, and those who have gone before them in the hate group. Remember socialization; people only know to hate because that's what they were told. I want you to read all of this from the CA Racist Skinheads which reads like the start of Hitler and the Nazi party.

Attention Patriots!! This upcoming June on Sunday the 26th in Sacramento, CA a gathering of Nationalists will merge and stand united under a single banner and for a single purpose! The Traditional Workers Party has become the voice of our people. **Adolf Hitler's first party was the National Socialist German Workers' Party.** *No other political party holds the views or interests of the Traditional European-American Family in the forefront of their agenda; in this the Traditional Workers Party stands apart. As Euro-Americans our voice has been all but silenced. Our cultures and traditions have been blatantly attacked and degenerated for countless generations at this point. Our borders here in America and all over Europe are constantly under-siege. The global elite have seemingly waged a war upon our people, without allowing us to fight back. The time for resistance is NOW! Caucasian people exist! We have the right to exist!! And we have the right to exist as Caucasian people!!! No longer will we sit aside and let alien cultures dictate our decline. We stand firm in our values and we do so united. So join us in Sacramento, CA.*

On behalf of all GSS, we hope to see everyone there. CA Racist Skinheads

Earlier I mentioned ignorance, and it is worth repeating. Ignorance is merely not knowing. People fear allowing others to know they are ignorant about something. Ignorance paralyzes people and stops them from learning; keeps them confined in their world. But by accident a person can discover what they don't know and share what they learned. A Caucasian male, Paul, came to my home to shoot a video for a commercial. He said he didn't know anything about diversity and inclusion, so he would enjoy making this video. It was fun, and it only took me four takes. As Paul was packing up, he said he did learn a lot plus he said my video was great. As I walked him to his truck, he turned to me and said, "We don't have to worry about diversity in our shop because everyone was a Caucasian male." That was a perfect opportunity for me to share my knowledge. I told him his organization is very diverse, and

I didn't know anything about them. I asked him these two questions: "Are all your co-workers the same age?" "Does everyone have the same skill level?" Paul answered no to both questions; I knew he would. I told him his office was very diverse. Paul paused for a moment and said, 'I never thought about it that way.' He said he was going to tell everyone at work about how diverse they were. There's nothing better than allowing someone to come to their own conclusions about diversity, fair treatment, and their willingness to learn.

Switching topics, a bit. Have you ever noticed how people in the workplace, school, mall, and other places eat with those who look like them? That's self-segregation. Is self-segregation good? I don't think there is a right or wrong answer to this question. It happens everywhere. We have black and white churches and black and white college fraternities and sororities. I've seen it and done it, so what should an organization or school do about it? In my job on the carrier and my last job I worked on self-segregation. On the carrier during chow, mealtime, I went to everyone's table to get acquainted and show them I had no favorites. When I went to certain tables, it was a frosty reception. Everyone looked at me as if I was crazy. I was not part of their regular group. I sat and started the conversation and eventually quite a few of them were chatty. Each department and work center sat together and dared not go to another table unless invited and that rarely happened. It was kind of funny to me at first, but it was basically a harmless practice. It did not help eliminate any stereotypes of each group but a few of them liked the stereotype they had.

At my last job, people were self-segregated by race, ethnicity, or less common their work area. We started brown bag lunches and I ensured there was diversity in the room. These lunches not only demonstrated that there was similar work issues everywhere in the organization but it got some more serious issues in front of or senior leadership. Some things did change because of the opportunity the brown bag lunches brought to everyone interested in change. I don't think self-segregation is wrong because it energizes some people and it provides a way for people to speak freely. However, self-segregation can be divisive and create a lack of trust. At some point, we need to start hanging out with those who don't look like us. We'll never know what that person could bring to our life. I'm fortunate that I traveled to different countries and experienced something magical in learning about those different than me.

CHAPTER 10

Hate

T HE BIG PINK ELEPHANT. Hate breeds all kinds of behaviors that are divisive. It is a powerful emotion and causes behaviors to be irrational and blinding. Hate takes a lot of energy. Imagine being tense, stressed, angry. Although some people who hate are happy to hate and love creating havoc. An honest discussion about hate rarely happens. Instead, people talk around hate. Therefore, rarely nothing changes if ever. Hate is an uncomfortable subject, so it is usually the big pink elephant in the room. Will anything change?

Racism, sexism, Islamophobia, and ethnicity bashing are fueled by hate. People, in general, do not like being accused of hate. Hate group members don't care if their accused of hate because that gives their group legitimacy, at least in their eyes. Hate group members don't see their behavior as hate rather it is a love of who they are that they are supporting. Most people do not like being called a racist either. And as you've probably heard, denial is not just a river in Egypt. So, until we talk honestly about hate and what to do we keep going around in circles.

So, what do we do about hate? Understand where the hate is coming from and start there. For instance, when I was talking to Sam from

Chapter 6 I asked him where his hate came from and he told me he first learned hate from his parents and grandparents. Another way to conquer hate is to be open to others' beliefs no matter what they are because that sets up a lively and beneficial conversation. When I was speaking to Steffan Chapter 4 about his beliefs before leaving the hate group, he told me how he hated blacks. That gave me ideas on what he and I should talk about and how I should approach our conversations. We talked about his hate and why he was talking to me. I had to have him tell me why he should hate me, the five why's. Steffan didn't make it to the third why. Additionally, you can stand up to hate by speaking out, in writing on websites or articles, calling out hate related behaviors, or stopping divisive actions. On the carrier there were quite a few epithets and inappropriate comments around me, I think they were testing me. I did what I had to do by calling out the bad behaviors even offering alternatives to what was said. You don't have to attend every argument you're invited to, great to remember when talking about hate. I was in a store shopping with my husband and while standing at the deli waiting to be served a Caucasian gentleman came up behind us. He yelled, "Hey boy" and I looked up and saw a young African-American man waving at this guy. Now, Caucasians sometimes call African-American men "boy" when they want to denigrate and humiliate them. The young man was not outwardly bothered but I was and I said to my husband, loud enough for the Caucasian gentleman to hear me, I hope he wasn't talking to the African-American young man because that's wrong. As my husband and I continue to shop the Caucasian gentleman walks up behind us and says people just need to love each other more. I say I agree and he says that he and the African-American young man know each other and that's how he speaks to him, then he gives a smile. I said it is not a very nice thing to say. He comes back with he's 72 years old and that's just how he speaks. I told him I understand but it didn't sound right. As my husband and I are trying to walk away he follows us and starts talking about race and how things are currently. I agreed with how sad things are about race and I said how we need to come together and talk. My husband and I keep shopping and as he continues to follow us around he finally said have a great holiday and I returned the wish. That was a necessary conversation for that gentleman so maybe just maybe he will think twice about how he greets his friend. These are not easy actions or conversations but easy is not always the answer especially when it comes to hate.

Hate allows some people to dominate others in any way they can. Extremists groups and Black Separatists use their hate to scare others. Extremists groups use a lot of rhetoric to instill fear in those they hate. They also commit horrible crimes and in some cases, commit murder. The killings committed are usually intended to get news coverage which will cause fear as well. They also like daring police to find them and bring them to justice which is just beginning to occur a bit more frequently. Each is a great scare tactic. The Ku Klux Klan (KKK) is the original hate group founded by six Confederate veterans on December 24, 1865, in Pulaski, TN. Their intent was to have a club for retired Confederate soldiers. They changed their minds and started hate crimes to intimidate and sometimes for their own entertainment. Their actions were public and often gruesome. That was the point, terrorize. Very few of the original KKK wore anything that masked their identity. Intimidation by flaunting who they were. The KKK member knew he would not face justice.

When there was a trial against a Caucasian person, again he had an all Caucasian jury who acquitted him.

Justice was hard to find for African-Americans accused of crimes because a jury was comprised of all Caucasians which at that time was not a jury of an African-American's peers. Here is an actual story to show

how the justice system was against African-Americans. His name is George Stinney, Jr. and he was electrocuted at 14 years old. In 1944, George was accused of brutally murdering two white girls ages 11 and 8. The two white girls had come by George's family house looking for certain types of flowers. George and his sisters told them they had no idea where to find those particular flowers. The two white girls went on their way and George and his sisters stayed in their yard. When the girls were found dead George was accused but the reason was unclear. But during that time, evidence was not needed to charge a Black person. He had a two-hour trial and the jury, all white, deliberated 10 minutes and convicted him of murder and he was sentenced to be executed. George's lawyer, a local political figure, refused to appeal and did not mount a defense. 84 days after their murders George was electrocuted. George was 5 feet tall and didn't weigh 100 lbs. He had to sit on telephone books, so his head reached the top of the chair. The straps were so big that when they threw the switch, his body convulsed, moving the large mask exposing his tearful face. Nothing but hate fueled George's treatment. To read the entire captivating story including his amazing exoneration 70 years later check out the Washington Post archives.. The legal system is still not where it should be especially for African-Americans. The number of African-Americans imprisoned based on the population is disproportionate to our population. The typical Caucasian answer for this is that African- Americans commit more crime based on statistics collected. The one thing I learned about statistics is you can make numbers say anything you want. Where is the crime data collected for these statistics? Neighborhoods and demographics matter when collecting crime statistics. Taking data from a known neighborhood for gangs will get higher crime numbers. Just like four out of five dentists prefer Crest toothpaste. Who are these four dentists? Do they work for Crest? Or do they get a lot of free stuff from Crest?

We sometimes hate what we fear. Many Caucasians feared, still do, African-Americans for numerous reasons. In the 1800s Caucasians feared African-American men around their women because they believed the African-American males would rape the women. This fear carried over to the 1900s and then another fear took hold. When African-Americans began to speak out and to fight back, Caucasians saw a determined group who were not giving in or up. The 2000s offered new race and ethnic dynamics. We are more diverse and sometimes more tolerant. There are more opportunities afforded minorities, but life is still not equitable. African-Americans do have more freedoms, many excellent education options, leadership opportunities at the highest levels, and so much more. Some Caucasians fear their loss of power and most importantly becoming irrelevant. The thought of becoming a minority in a country that "they feel they" built causes fear and fear easily leads to hate.

For some people, ignorance leads to hate. We fear what we don't know, and that does create hate for some. We usually don't try and find out for ourselves what we don't know. We rely on sources, some that are unreliable and have ulterior motives behind what they disseminate. We may not identify our fear as hate, but our behaviors show otherwise. Here's a great example. Very few U.S. citizens are familiar with and are much less friends with someone from the Middle East whether they are U.S. citizens or not. Ignorance of Islam and Muslims and their traditions causes fear; because we get some of our information from the media. Unfortunately, the only thing they know about someone from the Middle East or Muslim is that a lot of them are terrorists. And like any other race or ethnic group or religion a few who hate does not apply to everyone in the group. There are some hate groups from the South who are Christians, but they do some evil things. But that doesn't mean all or most Christians are haters. *All tigers are cats but not all cats are tigers.*

Unbiased education is part of what's missing. In Chapter 9 I told you about my two weeks with an Arab-American family and it was an awesome experience because I didn't know anything about Arab-Americans. That two weeks showed me I needed to approach others I didn't know very well without stereotypes. I had quite a few meals with the family, and was taught the difference between religion and culture. In only two weeks I learned some powerful information. I shared what I knew to educate others and to help stop the hate toward Islam and Muslims. The small number of people I can reach will not make a huge difference in reducing the hate toward Arab-Americans, but every bit of positive energy helps when fighting hate. The saying 'ignorance is bliss'. Is it really?

A true story about a seventeen-year old white male I'll call Cameron. I went home to my small town in Kentucky to do some training on race and how to deal with others who don't look like you. There had been many racial incidents and they asked me if I'd come home and do some training. I taught almost 400 middle, junior and senior high school students about race and hate. Cameron came to me, after I had taught a class and wanted to talk to me privately. Our conversation was a little over two and a half hours with a lot of silence at the beginning, during the first 45 minutes or so. He's a tall young man and very thin. Cameron's bangs flopped over his right eye so when he talked he had to use his hand to move his hair but a few times he hid behind his hair. We sat across from each other and I asked him what he wanted to talk about. He struggled to get the words out while looking down to the table. Almost a minute went by before he got the courage to say he had a problem calling Blacks nigger. He said he had tried to stop on his own, but he just couldn't. I had used that epithet during my training so I'm certain he was not quite sure how I might react to his words since we were talking one on one. Cameron was nervous talking to me. He kept his head down and would only glance up at me. I asked him to give me a background on why he started using that word. Cameron started using that word before he was ten. He said he heard his father say it frequently then and his father told him only negative things about Black people. Cameron called his father a racist and he didn't want to be like him which is one reason he desired to talk to me. He was socialized about Blacks so that's all he knew, he had no experience with a black person. When he was in grade school his family moved to a town that was a predominately black community. He was on edge throughout each school day. He explained he was uncomfortable at the school he attended with all the blacks around him. I believe he was ashamed about his next statements. The black guys he was around were usually calling each other nigger so he thought he could get in the conversation calling them nigger. But that doesn't work that way, whites can't use any form of the word nigger no matter what the connotation to blacks. He was confused about that. Many white people are confused when it comes to how blacks refer to each other using the word nigger but a white person. Some blacks use the word nigga to indicate someone is a friend but only blacks can use that word as well as nigger. Additionally, Cameron also noticed a few blacks fought a lot and he almost got caught up in fights himself. Fighting was just one of the negative traits Cameron's father told him about blacks which reinforced Cameron and why he kept calling them niggers.

Since moving away from the black community Cameron met blacks that did not fit his father's stereotypes. Cameron was pensive when he did look at me, so I knew he was sincere about changing his vocabulary and the way he thought about blacks. First, I needed him to feel comfortable with me and see that all blacks are not the stereotypes, and he can have a conversation with blacks. I started asking him questions from my Ask and Reveal list. That is a list I created of about 68 questions to use as conversation starters with people who don't look like you. I asked him some easy questions like what his favorite food was, then I told him mine, which spawned other questions thus a conversation began. Cameron seemed surprised at how easy we started a conversation. I asked him if he would use the questions if I sent them to him and he said yes. He told me he liked being on the computer, so I asked him what kind of things he did on his computer, another easy but interactive conversation began. Cameron became more relaxed with me and he even started making eye contact, he smiled a bit, and at one point he got a small laugh in. I felt great because Cameron was more relaxed, and he said I showed him that not all blacks are the same. *All tigers are cats but not all cats are tigers.* If Cameron wants to change, which I believe he does, he will give the questions a try although I'm sure he has some fear about the process. It's not as easy as it sounds. He was eager to get the list of questions and I told him I would check on him periodically. He gave me his email address although he said he doesn't really email but I told him I would email him anyway in case he did want to talk. I did email him, and it took some coaxing for him to email me back. He hadn't tried the list of questions yet. Cameron said he was going to ask some questions he just needed a bit more confidence. He doesn't email me back, but I still send him emails.

We all have biases so we all have prejudices. Once we admit to that, it is a bit easier to talk about how hate develops. Hate prohibits the possibilities to enrich our personal lives by getting to know a person different than ourselves beyond their favorite food or a religious holiday. Without the familiarity of others, haters will continue to wreak havoc.

The Attitude Behavior Cycle displays how our prejudices affect others and a great way to work on ending prejudices. This happens daily because we are all socialized with bias.

I'll use the example with the teacher from Chapter 1. Using the cycle above: A Caucasian teacher has a room full of students half Caucasian and the other half minorities, mainly African-American. The teacher believes African-American children are not as devoted to doing their homework, not as intelligent, are lazy in class, and just don't care about education. The teacher was socialized that way. She has a very negative attitude about African-American students and treats them that way. She rarely calls on them in class, she doesn't check their homework as thoroughly, she spends less time with them in class. The teacher feels all that would be a waste of time. I'm the African-American student and I don't do my homework regularly, I talk to my friends during class, and display a general negative attitude. My negative attitude causes me to behave as above. That's how the cycle works, attitude affects behavior, affects attitudes, affects behaviors and on it goes. The Cycle is unforgiving and relentless. Notice values are identified as being crucial to developing attitudes in the Cycle. Attitudes such as hate in the U.S. has been part of who we are from the beginning of our settling of this country in 1492. Hate toward the Native Americans was justified by rationalizing that they were natives and ignorant of what real life was about. The European Caucasians never took the time to find out about the Native Americans and how they had survived.

There's no way hate is going to disappear anytime soon unless we do something about it; act. It takes courage and strength, mentally and physically, to combat hate. We must do this someday. We must combat hate. What better time than now? We must do this now because some day is not a day on the calendar.

CHAPTER 11

"I have 10 African-American friends"

HERE'S SOME TRUTH ABOUT RACE. I grew up in a small town, about 500 people, in Western Kentucky. My extended family was the only African-Americans in town, and there were about 31 of us. The honest talk about race for me started when I was in grade school. One of my Caucasian friends asked me intriguing questions such as 'what color is my blood', or 'why is your hair that way.' Believe it or not some touched my hair to check it out. Here's the best question, 'why is your skin brown?' These questions were not meant to degrade or insult me they were honest questions about something they did not know. We were young and since we were friends those questions were not threatening. Remember ignorance causes many conversations about race to be awkward. After I answered their questions we just kept moving forward. Of course, I practically knew everything about my Caucasian friends because that's what they teach in school and they were all around me. Some might find those questions insensitive and unnecessary, but curiosity got the best of them. And I was different. While playing softball in my early teens we would travel to tournaments and sometimes we went places that they hated people who look like me.

It was obvious they did not want me there. I was our pitcher, and a good one, so I was upfront easy to see. I was called nigger more than once.

In addition, there came the words porch monkey and these people were very loud, and they wanted me gone. We just made sure we beat their team and we did.

When we got into high school, and I was subjected to hate, still not from my school mates. I was curious about something, so I asked my friends this question. I asked my friends if Caucasians don't like Blacks then why do they spend so much time getting a tan? There was no good answer and I still don't know. If we can talk to whites about how good their tans are then why not talk to us with our beautiful complexions? Race is still an awkward conversation and the most awkward conversations are about African-Americans and Caucasians. There are also heated conversations about Latinos/Hispanics and people from the Middle East, Africa and the usual suspects. These conversations usually begin with a stereotype or some dramatic claim. We must change our discussions on race to more educational, funny, entertaining, and prolific.

Too many blacks and whites have not moved on from the 1800's, and there cannot be much movement forward while reaching back. Things like lack of diversity in many businesses, unequal quality education, privilege, and just plain hate hamper forward momentum. There are so many missed opportunities to have an honest dialogue about race and it's unfortunate that happens. Being politically correct also hinders an open discussion for a couple of reasons. The sarcasm that many people use for being politically correct can create tension and lead to being uncomfortable.

People rationalize why they are uncomfortable about discussions of race. They say, 'I'm not racist, I have ten African-American friends,' as though there is a magical number to prove someone is not a racist. Instead of counting the number of friends you have why not talk about the type of relationship you have with your 10 African- American friends. But this is not one-sided. There are plenty of blacks who hate whites as well. Blacks don't count the number of white friends. Here's another rationalization. "I don't see color." That sounds great except the context in which the statement is made, we're talking about color. I've heard that many of times when a discussion of race comes up and instead of having an insightful conversation about race, there's no reason to continue the discussion; there's no color. Most people I know are proud of their color, I know I am. Saying "I don't see color" is like saying he or she doesn't see me. So, if you are trying to say you don't judge based on color then say that so a great conversation can start.

Discussions about race get sidetracked because someone is concerned about being Politically Correct (PC) as described above. In an earlier chapter, I explained the reason PC inhibits constructive conversations about race. When we can learn to be respect towards each other we can talk about race in a meaningful way.

Affirmative Action (AA) is also a reason why talking about race is awkward because it is a misunderstood subject and it is a popular one. Remember AA has negative connotations because leaders widely misused it and made it about racial quotas. The true use of AA is when a person from a protected class applies to college, is up for promotion in their organization, or desires to join the police forces, is given special consideration because of historically unfair treatment. For example, when a Caucasian male and an African-American female are applying for the same job, and their resumes are virtually equal, then Affirmative Action can happen, and they can justifiably hire the African-American female. Unfortunately, Caucasians can suffer illegal discrimination under the AA plan. Some call that reverse discrimination but if someone is treated differently because of race, ethnicity, sex, etc. it is discrimination. One of the most recent past publicized cases of this involves a

Caucasian female applying to the University of Michigan (UM) and she was not accepted, but UM admitted two African-American students. The following information is from the National Public Radio website.

The pivotal case, Grutter v. Bollinger, involved the university's law school. Barbara Grutter, who is Caucasian, applied for admission there in 1996. She was rejected. She investigated and found out that African-Americans and ethnic minorities who had lower overall admissions scores were admitted. Grutter sued, saying she was a victim of illegal discrimination. https://www.npr.org/news/specials/michigan/

The Supreme Court decided that the University's Law School could keep using the Affirmative Action plan, but the undergraduate program could not use AA. This case along with one in Texas started conversations about race, and it prompted other universities to examine their Affirmative Action policies. President John F. Kennedy signed Executive Order 10925 adding the Affirmative Action plan to equal opportunity because there were some inequities African-Americans experienced in many areas. Unfortunately, some of those same inequities are still occurring.

Of course, the quality of your friends and friendships should be more important than the number of friends you have.

CHAPTER 12

It's A Right-Handed World

"**Y**OU'RE OUT IN LEFT FIELD!"
I'm right-handed which means I am part of a club that rules everything. , being right-handed when
I shop for notebooks, all I do is go to the store and look for notebooks. I choose a color and pay. I played softball, so I needed a glove. I went to the sporting goods store, went to the gloves section, picked one out I loved and paid. I didn't even think about it. It was so easy to get my glove. I knew my glove was going to be available because I'm right-handed. It is a right-handed world. It's just how the world works. I didn't ask to be right-handed I just am. If I had been left-handed, I couldn't just walk in and choose any glove. To be fair, there are not many left-handed people, the minority, so they are not catered to because it is not feasible to devote a whole section for a left-handed glove. For my computer, I wanted a cordless mouse. I found the mouse section and just chose a color and paid. It's a right-handed world.

I have privilege because everything is for right-handers. I don't ask for a "right-handed" anything; it is easy to find because it's normal. I didn't earn this privilege, nor did I ask for it, it was given to me because

I am right-handed, in the majority. This privilege gives me an advantage every day. Even a coffee cup doesn't allow a left-handed person to see what's on the cup because it's a regular cup, for right-handed people to enjoy. Privilege is awesome. Everyone knows I'm right-handed, it's easy to see when I use my hands, and that's what makes it even better. Our culture is right-handed, and that establishes what is regular what's expected. Left- handed people are awkward. How many people have said, 'she's out in left field on that issue.', which is not an affirmative statement.

What if left-handed people began to be unreasonable? Left-handed people start saying it is not their fault they are left-handed and deserve to be treated just like right-handers. They claim that right-handers had an advantage because everything is structured made for them. It's not right.

Right-handed people get tired of hearing the same old thing from left-handers, "It's not fair." Or "Why do we have to be in a special section?" But things have progressed over the years for left-handers, so now they can find something for themselves a little easier. There's a Left-Handed store so they've moved up. Righties don't understand what else lefties want. Again, it's not my fault I'm right-handed.

This right-hand privilege is the work of Dr. Steven Jones, CEO of Jones and Associates Consulting. The Right Hand of Privilege It is an excellent way to reveal how privilege works.

Unearned privilege is real and needs to be recognized. Acknowledging that he or she receives favor without asking is a step in the right direction. Caucasian males receive the most privilege in our society. However, Caucasian women also have some privilege. For instance, Caucasian women find plenty of hair and facial care products in most every store, but not so for minorities and there is not much selection. White men have privilege in almost all areas of life just like right-handers. The following three examples show how white privilege affects different parts of minority life.

While I was in the Navy, I traveled a lot in the U.S. No matter where I went, I could always be sure of two things. One, there would be no African-American hair care products in the hotel. Two, no African- American skin care products, i.e. lotions, facial care. I realize the African-American population in the U.S. as of 2015 by the Census Bureau, is only 13.3%. But the buying power is over $1.2 Trillion dollars. Initially, it does not appear to be very economical to carry African-American care products but, a business never knows how many African-Americans do not stay at a hotel, or shop at a store because there are no products for us.

One actual Navy story happened on a base outside the U.S. African-American females stationed there could only find one African-American hair care product. It was like being left-handed. The one place it should have been was on base in the exchange store. They carry items from the

U.S. that Sailors would not usually find outside the U.S. It is convenience. It was not convenient for black females. What did the black female Sailors do? First, they had family send them the products they needed. Then, they voiced their displeasure to the right people and soon after more variety of black female hair care products were stocked. Now, what does this have to do with white privilege? African-American hair care products were different, unusual, not the norm and didn't have the privilege of stocked hair care products. Caucasian females did have the privilege for their hair care products to be stocked, unless it was special, the products were always there.

Here's the final example of privilege. A Caucasian male is looking to buy a home. He can choose to live in the very exclusive all Caucasian gated community or the poorest neighborhood he can find without a second thought. An African-American male would have to seriously think about living in the all-white gated community. His thoughts, "Will I be welcomed in the gated community?" "Will I have to move in a few days because of issues?" White privilege allowed the Caucasian to have a range of places to live while the African-American male had a range but there are questions. I've had some second thoughts about going certain places, particularly in the South, and some in the north, with Caucasians. Since my husband is white I do go places where there are all white people and I'm the only black person. I enjoy the opportunity to be around those different than me even though it might be a bit uncomfortable.

White privilege does exist. No one is blaming a Caucasian person for their privilege but he or she must own it when it occurs. Here are a couple of ideas to alleviate privilege. Acknowledge it when it happens. People who give privilege may do it unintentionally, so feedback will only help. Minorities being bold about white privilege can make real differences.

'Absolute power corrupts absolutely' is part of a quote by *John Emerich Edward Dalberg Acton, first Baron Acton* (1834–1902). He was called Lord Acton. White privilege gives absolute power. The quote actually reads, "Power tends to corrupt, and absolute power corrupts absolutely." That's not true with all powerful people.

With privilege comes power. Many Caucasians have privilege, and they have power. CEOs, governors, mayors, district attorneys, Chiefs of Police, University presidents, high school teachers, Presidents of the United States, and so much more. Caucasians predominantly hold these power positions.

The discussion of White Privilege is not intended to be negative. Its intent is to bring something to light that may not be recognized. No one can blame white males for having white privilege. The issue is white males enjoy their privilege at others' expense. Be vocal about the good ole' boys network. That's white privilege on steroids.

White privilege is real.

CHAPTER 13

Perception

YOUR PERCEPTION IS YOUR REALITY. Your perspective affects your perception. Hate distorts perception. That's important to understand when talking about hate. Everyone's coming from their view of the situation. We believe our view is the right one based on what we know. Another person does the exact same thing and that's when conflict happens.

I'll start with a hypothetical situation to explain what I mean. Imagine in your living room there appeared a huge diamond. It must be a big one. A very clear and bright diamond. Your family members and friends would stand around the diamond from different areas in your living room to check it out. Everyone in the living room will see different colors, sparkles, views, cuts and more. Same diamond different perspectives so their perceptions are very different but again it's the same diamond. Hate is like a flaw in a diamond.

Different perceptions cause discontentment leading to conflicts. Conflicts can get out of hand if a person doesn't realize some one sees the same thing differently. True example between my husband and I about NASCAR being a real sport. I wasn't a NASCAR fan until I met my husband. He said the drivers had to be in shape to sit in a hot car for hours while driving at 190mph, but he does have some air blowing on him. He also has two helpers in his ears always, spotter and crew chief. I said let's look at a tennis player. They need stamina because they are in the hot sun or rain, without any type of air blowing on him or her, and it's only them out there no crew chief to help. My husband's come back was a tennis player is only concentrating on one person while at 190mph a NASCAR driver must contend with those cars around him driving for a win. I didn't want to give in, but I said I can see how NASCAR can be called a sport, but a tennis player is a true athlete. I changed my perspective and then my perception of NASCAR drivers changed. He agreed about tennis, reluctantly.

Here's another real example that may be a bit weird and hard to grasp initially but think about the diamond example. Police/Sheriffs see a traffic stop as the law. An African-American male most likely sees a traffic stop as a possible crime scene with him the victim. There's no common ground except an African-American male knows it's the law to make legal traffic stops. This is not easy an easy situation. One solution that's working in neighborhoods is community policing. I see police with young kids in the neighborhood, but they are not the age, driving cars. A one-day Police Academy for young adults is one way to start developing trust with each other. Both sides explain their view of the diamond. Establish trust even though trust is hard to earn. Start with truth. If the only time they see a law enforcement professional is when they are pulled over then nothing changes. Trust will come but it is not an overnight thing and I believe some people think it is. It can happen.

Another prevailing perception is without immigrants some people would have jobs. The perspective is immigrants should leave our country. What's interesting about this perception is the jobs mentioned have always been available, but no one wanted those jobs until the immigrants took them. Truthfully, the jobs immigrants do are not prestigious, nor do they normally pay a lot. A lot of service jobs. Honestly, I'm not sure if the jobs immigrants currently do were made available that those complaining would start working. It's easier to blame others for the things we don't do but could. It's just easier to complain.

Unfortunately, we can't see exactly what someone else sees. So, there must be give and take to bridge the gaps in our perspectives. How does that happen? Acknowledgement that the differences can be bridged. Do not worry about who gives in first. Listen, actively listen. Take real time to think about what the others are saying and more than just a couple of hours. Be willing to admit when a valid point is made and have courage to make a change in your perspective. Be eager to see things from a different perspective. One consideration about perspective and is a person's direct or indirect experience with the situation. If he or she has been there done that they may be more inclined to change perspective. Someone who has indirect experience may be more resistant to a perspective change because their own perspective is not fully developed.

We perceive everything. It's our senses working together to give us the way we experience the world. Think about that.

CHAPTER 14

The Others

THERE IS ONE AREA that I hinted to about religion and hate groups in Chapter 8. Islam is not the only religion that is associated with hate, but it is the biggest and most effective at causing fear.

As stated in Chapter 8, there are many who don't even know the five pillars of Islam much less why they are committing terrorists' acts for Islam. I've chosen three different organizations who believe in God and interpret their holy word in their own way.

First is Westboro Baptist Church in Topeka, KS. Their belief is that homosexuality is against the Bible and will be the downfall of the world. They were at one-time particularly interested in the military. Westboro would riot military funerals with signs like "God Hates Fags." Their belief was the military who were killed, particularly troops in Afghanistan and Iraq, was God's way at justice for homosexuality. Additionally, at one time they were very vocal and some thought very disrespectful to the fallen soldiers families because they would picket funerals.

Another religion is Kingdom Identity Ministries (KIM). They call themselves politically incorrect with outreach ministries. Additionally, they believe they are God's race, true Israel, white people, and European people. They are out in Harrison, AR. Their online activity is their main communication medium. KIM has written quite a few what they call catalogs and there's one for children. That is a smart technique, teach hate from the beginning of a child's life and that's all they know. KIM is not the first hate group to obviously teach hate from childhood. Kingdom Identity Ministries even take donations.

The final religious ideology is from America's Promise Ministries out of Phoenix, AZ. Their whole focus is teaching the truth about Jesus Christ, His people, kingdom and more. They take parts of Bible verses and put them together to make their point. Now there are a couple more groups worth mentioning that are not religious.

The Tradionalist Worker Party (TWP) is out of Cincinnati, OH. They claim to be the first political organization created by and for working families. TWP is a local type party trying to fight being in the global community. They believe White Americans have been abandoned by the system. White children are a real concern for them and they are working to ensure a future for white children. The 14 Words are perfect here. "We must secure the existence of our society and a future for white children."

One more interesting group I recently discovered. Kool Kids Klub (KKK) is a way for kids to have something to belong to and have positive activities with each other. Kool Kids Klub has t-shirts to show they belong to a kool group. But the more recognized version of the Kool Kids Klub relates to the Klu Klux Klan. All over the internet, including social media, Kool Kids Klub members wear their own shirts that have the original KKK doctrine. There is difference between the KKK t-shirts as the racist propaganda one is *3 K's a day keeps the minorities away*. This Kids Klub is like the concept of the Hitler youth. Adolf knew he needed leaders to keep the Third Reich going so he indoctrinated them as Hitler youth. Of course, they all had blonde hair and blue eyes. The perfect Aryans. Once again start them early they'll probably stay the course.

These types of groups are most vibrant in their local community but can lure people into their beliefs from afar. Although these groups are small does not mean they are not as ruthless as a large group like ISIS. We can't ignore hate from anyone anywhere.

CHAPTER 15

What Disguise Do You Wear?

WE NEVER TRULY KNOW who we meet and his or her behaviors may not be who they really are because of a disguise. So how do we figure out if the person is wearing a disguise? You must first figure out why they wear it. There are four disguises that almost anyone can and will wear when the situation presents itself. Power, it's easier, to impress, and concealment.

There are so many reasons why someone would wear a disguise. One reason is power. Power disguises are worn to get power or to give it away. Who gives power away on purpose? A person not comfortable with having power and don't like the consequences associated with failure. For instance, Ray is a very skilled technician but is not comfortable being a supervisor because of his poor communication. You can get power by showing power. Sylvia feels she's ready for more responsibility and power, so she always takes charge whenever the opportunity comes up. She exudes confidence and soon her supervisors notice and promote her, and she gets legitimate power.

For some it's easier to wear a disguise than be themselves. There's nothing wrong with who they are but for some reason they feel their true persona would not be accepted. I've worn a disguise as a timid female because I didn't think I would be accepted into a group being a strong female.

Impressing others is another reason to wear a disguise. Dale believes

What Disguise Do You Wear?

he must impress Jill's parents because one is a doctor the other is a state senator. Jill already told him to be himself and her parents would love him. Dale isn't taking any chances, so he buys a brand new suit, shoes, and gets a fresh haircut. He's also practicing how to introduce himself.

Concealment is always a good reason to wear a disguise. Some may desire to keep their true selves hidden away until the right moment and then reveal him or herself. Concealing oneself from others seems sneaky and wrong but people have their reasons. Sometimes concealment is self-preservation.

Of course, no one must wear the same disguise all the time and probably does not. Changing or not wearing disguises is situational as the previous examples showed. But before a person decides to wear a disguise he or she should take a breath and determine if they need a disguise. When I decided to be myself as a strong female I weighed my options and knew being myself I was at my best. The decision to be myself wasn't easy so be prepared to possibly be unsure about who you should be in certain situations. Sometimes when we are being ourselves we are assessed by others and told what we are not, but it is worth this scrutiny to be yourself. One way to avoid wearing a disguise is to be honest with yourself, know who you are always and don't listen to just anyone who tries to tell you who you are.

Fear nothing. There's no reason to fear being not good enough not being right or not being enough. I bet you got where you are in life by being bold and fearing nothing. Why would you need a disguise? Take time to breakdown the situation to deliver an appropriate response without fear. You know who you are.

Why not be tenacious instead of wearing a disguise? If someone tries to make you wear a disguise through their words or actions get tenacious. Tell those who are saying you're not good enough that they are not good enough to make judgment on you. Tenacity has proven very effective for me and should be a go to way not to wear a disguise.

Finally, integrity means everything. Once a person says what they plan to do just do it. Here's one definition of integrity I like. Integrity is doing the right thing when no one is looking. If you are doing that then you don't need a disguise.

Let's be honest. We will wear a disguise to fit into a group or to stave away embarrassment. I've worn many disguises, but I hated doing that because I was not being my true self. One time I didn't wear a disguise was when confronting hate and racists. I needed to show who I really was and keep my focus on the task at hand and not what disguise I was going to wear. Being real when dealing with hate is the only effective way hate can be overcome.

CHAPTER 16

'Let's Be Real!'

WHEN WE'RE IN A SETTING with people we know, like and think the way we do we feel comfortable talking. We would probably say something around close friends that you would not say in public. I've been guilty more than once. Does that mean I am a bad person? No. But I should be mindful of what I say because I might slip and say the wrong thing. Let's be real about the things we say or hear.

Have you ever been in a room with a mixed group of people and someone tells a Hispanic/Latino joke? What do you do? I've been there. This is how I handled it because I wanted it to be a teachable moment. Of course, as EOA I take the fun out of the room. My go to response when someone said something offensive was, "What does that mean?". I still use it because it is so good. Everyone looks at me like I had three heads. Then silence. So, I asked again, "What does that mean?" Everyone starts saying 'you know what it means, we are only joking. We're not the only ones who laugh about that and there's no one here that could be offended so no problem.' We sometimes assume that because the object of the "joke "is not around everyone else is okay with what is said. Not true. Where's the integrity? Sounds like a good argument but how do they know everything about everyone there in the room. And it only sounds good if you always talk that way. I told them that was amazing that's all they knew to say about Hispanics/Latinos in this example. They really didn't like that comment. I added unless they have walked in Hispanic/Latino skin how could they know anything. It's not enough to walk around in someone else's shoes but to walk around in their skin. That's a perspective that can change many assumptions, beliefs, stereotypes, and biases.

Have you ever been in a group and someone said something about a nigger? That word is usually a conversation stopper except when amongst friends. This word will probably never go away because hate will never go away. Our socialization will keep hate alive. Unfortunately, a reason nigger stays around is because some African-Americans use it and a form of this word 'nigga' that blacks say means friend or a friendly greeting. Since the word nigga is different it's okay to use it. Right? All that has done is make it okay to say nigger or to call someone that name. Additionally, only African-Americans can use nigga, so it makes it as controversial as nigger. That's how it is explained. How does a word change meaning because it is said by a person who does not belong to a particular group? There is no reasonable response. So, people see a double standard and believe either it's okay for everyone to say or no one to say. Nigga keeps us divided. I've been one of the people who has said either everyone uses it, or no one does. That is not popular but it's the only way we can respect each other.

Have you ever been in a room when someone makes a disparaging remark about Muslims? Terrorist is probably most common. Muslims have really come under fire because of all the terrorists' attacks. Calling every Muslim, a terrorist is not appropriate either. Islamic State in Iraq and Syria (ISIS) has made a worldwide impact especially their recruitment success. As I stated earlier, ISIS is a jihadist group which are extremists Muslims. A little education can help stop disparaging remarks, stereotypes, biases, and hate. The contrast to make the point is most hate group members in the U.S. are extreme thinking Bible Belt Protestants. So does that mean every Protestant belongs to a hate group or call them Neo-Nazis or Skinheads? When I made that analogy, people begin to think differently. The headpiece men wear is actually called Kalansuwa, Turban, Imamah, Shemagh and Keffiyeh and is used for sun protection and religious obligation. Western culture is making a fashion impact on some Middle Eastern males. When they leave their country, they change their traditional head wear for fashionable hats.

Remember all tigers are cats but not all cats are tigers. Using disparaging comments about or toward people only shows a person's ignorance and possible arrogance.

CHAPTER 17

Bag It

"I CAN'T BELIEVE I SAID THAT!"

Sometimes it's hard to keep our feelings from becoming our words. Even with all my training and experience I spill my bag all over the floor occasionally. Your bag is your safety net when it comes to stereotypes and biases. A paper bag filled with something heavy, rocks or marbles will work as a symbol for alleviating microaggressions, insulting words, stereotypes and hate. Microaggressions are not only racial they are sexist, also religious, include sexual orientation, new to the list is Islamophobia, and there is much more. Here's how the bag works. You get a paper bag and some rocks, marbles or something heavy and place one in the bag for each stereotype, bias, or thought of hate. Keep the bag someplace where you can see it to remind you of what you have put away and keep it closed. This is a test of your integrity. You know what you put away and see if you can keep this bag closed, keep your hate to yourself. This can be done for a group as well, which is how I use it the most. Whether you are alone or in a group the process is the same. When doing this alone you first think about your obvious stereotypes and biases that are easily identified. For instance, I know

I am prejudice against Purple people. Then I put one object in my bag. I put the prejudice away. My bag was heavy, and I've taken it with me whenever I moved, and I still have it today.

In a group I must make it okay for group members to put rocks in their bags by showing them or giving them a list races, ethnicities, religions, etc. Using this process with groups help them be more honest with themselves without anyone knowing.

Close your bags and keep them close as a reminder that you put away those stereotypes, prejudices, and biases. When the bag is seen often that helps keep it closed. Inevitably figuratively you will spill your bag all over the floor. It's out there, all your rocks so now what. It takes courage to explain why you said it, but you must reconcile the differences in your behavior. I've had my bag spill all over a few floors. I make it sound simple to pick up your rocks when they spill but it is not. From my experience, apologize, admit it, explain a bit of why it happened, and let them know you are trying to change. That last sentence may seem useless, but it can change the atmosphere from intense to tense. It was not always easy to bounce back from my bag spill, but it made me a better person in many ways.

This is the perfect time to talk about SEE again from Chapter 6. Surely, you've heard people say, "That changed my life." What causes that feeling is a Significant Emotional Event (SEE). Anyone can have a SEE at any time. Because we are diverse what causes a SEE for one person may not be so for another. If you remember in Chapter 1 I wrote about the socialization process. It's how you develop your beliefs, values, language and learn your religion and culture. Imagine something so emotional that it could change your behaviors, beliefs, stereotypes, and prejudices. That's a SEE. We just don't casually change our beliefs or prejudices. A SEE can change the contents of your bag and hopefully make it lighter.

AND FINALLY...

HATE IS A PROGRESSIVE DISEASE. I saw it up close and personal and it is ugly. Hate is very emotional and blurs, distorts, reality. It takes so much energy to constantly think about hate, write about it, rally about it, march about it, yell about it, all of those keep emotions high. Don't let their smiles fool you. Behind those smiles are calculating minds and hearts. Ignorance and fear create hate in us and they are both passed on and on through socialization. We see people as we want to see them vice seeing people as who they really are. We must take care that we treat people with respect. It's not always easy to do that but with determination and openness it works. Trust me I know.

CPSIA information can be obtained
at www.ICGtesting.com
Printed in the USA
LVHW05s1428220918
590859LV00006B/54/P